MW01600565

ME *AND* JESUS
A JOURNEY OF FAITH

BY

J.W. CROMER

FIRST EDITION, 2025

Me and Jesus: A Journey of Faith
Copyright © 2025 by **J.W. Cromer**

All rights reserved. No part of this publication may be reproduced, stored in a retrieval system, or transmitted in any form or by any means—electronic, mechanical, photocopying, recording, or otherwise—without the prior written permission of the publisher, except in the case of brief quotations used in reviews or articles.

ISBN (Paperback): 979-8-9999588-0-8
ISBN (eBook): 979-8-9999588-1-5

Published by **Christ International Inc.**
Crab Orchard, Kentucky, USA

Unless otherwise indicated, Scripture quotations are taken from the Holy Bible, King James Version.

Cover design by J.W. Cromer

Printed in the United States of America

Dedication

To Jesus Christ—
the Alpha and Omega,
the Author and Finisher of my faith,
the Lamb who was slain,
and the risen King of glory.
This book is not mine, but Yours.
Every step of my journey,
every testimony written here,
every prayer whispered in weakness,
and every victory won in faith—
they all belong to You.
You are the One who called me out of darkness
and into Your marvelous light.
You are the Good Shepherd
Who left the ninety-nine to find me.
You are the Rock beneath my feet,
the Refuge in every storm,
and the Living Water that has never failed me.
May every word in these pages magnify Your Name,
every testimony exalt Your mercy,
and every reader encounter Your presence.
If there is any beauty in these lines,
it is Yours.

If there is any power,
it is Your Spirit.
If there is any glory,
let it rise to You alone.
I bow this offering at the foot of the Cross.
May it be acceptable in Your sight,
a witness to the world
that You are still the same yesterday,
today,
and forever.
*"Unto him that loved us,
and washed us from our sins in his own blood,
And hath made us kings and priests unto God and his Father;
to him be glory and dominion for ever and ever.
Amen."*
—Revelation 1:5–6

Acknowledgments

Above all, I give glory and thanks to my Lord and Savior, Jesus Christ. He is the true Author of this story, the One who called me to walk by faith, and the reason these pages exist. Without Him, there would be no testimony to share.

To my precious wife, Anissa—thank you for walking beside me with prayer and patience. Your faith has strengthened me more than words can say, and your encouragement has been a light in this journey.

I thank Martina Lucas for her dedication and for getting me started when the call to write this book first came. She stood with me in those uncertain early days, helping me take the first steps when the task felt bigger than I was. Her support and encouragement became a spark that God used to ignite the flame of obedience in my heart, and for that, I am grateful.

I would also like to thank Sammy and Danny Ford for their encouragement, guidance, and understanding—for allowing me to take weeks off at a time and covering for me while I was away. They are more than friends or cousins—they are my brothers. They do what they say they will do, and their loyalty has been a gift I treasure deeply.

I also want to acknowledge Dr. Todd Michael Fink, his wife, Letsy, and their sons, Joel and Logan. Their ministry in the Holy Land and their Missions to Mexico have been an inspiration and a blessing to me. Their obedience to the call of Christ and their labor for the Gospel are a shining witness of faith in action.

I give thanks as well to the many young missionaries I have met and spoken with throughout Israel. Your prayers and prophetic words were like living water along the way. To each stranger God placed in my path who became a good friend—thank you. To the elders who placed fresh vegetables, bread, and water in my hands, even when they had little themselves—you were Christ's kindness in my wilderness. Each of you was a blessing when I felt far from home. Through you, the Lord reminded me that He has many friends in many cities, towns, and villages.

Finally, to those unseen and unnamed who have prayed, encouraged, or helped in ways only God and eternity will fully reveal—I thank you. May the Lord reward your faithfulness, and may this book be a small part of the harvest He is bringing forth.

"Therefore, my beloved brethren, be ye stedfast, unmoveable, always abounding in the work of the Lord, forasmuch as ye know that your labour is not in vain in the Lord"
—1 Corinthians 15:58.

CONTENTS

FOREWORD

By Anissa Cromer

There's something refreshingly rare about my husband, Jeff Cromer. He doesn't just believe the Word—he lives it. He doesn't just talk about faith—he walks it. And he doesn't just teach obedience—he actually does what the Lord says, even when it costs him something, even when it makes no earthly sense.

Over the course of this book, you'll walk with Jeff through airports, ancient cities, valleys, waterfalls, and mountaintops—but what's even more remarkable is that you'll also walk with him into the heart of God. You'll see what it looks like when someone refuses to lean on human understanding and instead listens fully to the voice of the Holy Spirit. You'll feel the discomfort of letting go of control—and the deep peace that follows surrender. You'll see the beauty of divine appointments, the mystery of God's timing, and the unmistakable fingerprints of Jesus on every page.

Jeff is not a polished theologian or a trained missionary. He's a man from Kentucky with a Bible in his backpack and a fire in his heart. He's someone who said "yes" to God without knowing the destination—who stepped into a land of promise with nothing but trust in his Provider. That kind of faith changes you. And it's changing those who hear his story.

As his wife, I've had the privilege of walking alongside Jeff through the process of bringing this book to life. I've seen the tears, the prayers, the wrestlings, and the worship that went into these pages. What you'll read here isn't exaggerated or embellished. It's raw. It's real. And it's overflowing with the presence of the Lord.

This isn't just Jeff's story—it's an invitation. An invitation to listen more closely, to obey more quickly, to walk more freely, and to believe again that God still leads those who are willing to follow Him.

So settle in. Open your heart. And get ready to be stirred, challenged, and encouraged.

Because this story isn't about a man. It's about the God who still parts seas, speaks through strangers, heals hearts, and leads His people—one step of faith at a time.

—Anissa Cromer

PREFACE

When the Lord first placed it on my heart to write this book, I wrestled with Him. I felt unqualified. I wasn't a trained theologian, a published author, or someone who had all the answers neatly packaged in a notebook. I was simply a man from Kentucky with a Bible, a backpack, and a burning call to say "yes" to Jesus—wherever He would lead me.

But the Lord reminded me of something: He has never been looking for polished vessels, only willing ones. He used shepherd boys, fishermen, farmers, and prophets who often felt weak, uncertain, or unworthy. And yet, when they yielded, God's strength was made perfect in their weakness.

This book is not about me. It's about what happens when an ordinary man says "yes" to an extraordinary God. It's about what it looks like to live by faith when there is no plan, no safety net, no backup. It's about hearing His voice in the middle of airports, deserts, valleys, mountains, and crowded city streets—and learning to trust that His hand is steady even when my steps are not.

As you read these pages, you will find stories of divine appointments, sacred places, and moments of both trial and triumph. You will see the fingerprints of Jesus in the details, the Spirit's leading in the timing, and the Father's faithfulness in every provision. My prayer is that these testimonies stir something deep within you—not admiration for me, but fresh hunger for Him.

I pray you will be challenged to listen more closely, to obey more quickly, and to walk more freely in the Spirit. If the Lord can lead me across oceans and through ancient lands without a map, a plan, or even a phone, then He can certainly lead you in the details of your life. He is still the same God who called Abraham out of Ur, Moses up Mount Sinai, Elijah to Mount Carmel, and the disciples to leave everything behind and follow Jesus.

This is not just a book of stories. It is an invitation. An invitation to trust that God still speaks, still guides, and still has a plan that is far better than anything we could design on our own.

So, before you turn the page, I ask one thing: open your heart. Let these words point you past me and toward the One who is worthy of it all. If by the end of this book you are not only encouraged, but compelled to step out in faith, then I will know my obedience in writing has fulfilled its purpose.

Because this journey isn't really mine—it's His.

—J.W. Cromer

CHAPTER 1

The Call and the Altar

There's a stirring that begins deep in the soul when God speaks. Sometimes it's thunder. Other times, it's a whisper that refuses to go away. That's how this book began—not with ambition, but with obedience.

For years, people would tell me, "You need to write a book." It usually came after I spoke at a church or shared a story about something the Lord had done—especially stories from Israel. I'd smile and respond, "God already gave us a Book—but not many people read it."

But something shifted. My wife, Anissa, looked at me one day and said, "Jeff, if you write a book, God could use it to lead people to Him, which would bring the people back to His Scriptures." Her words sank deep, and they wouldn't let go.

Still, I wrestled with the idea. *Who am I?*

I've never attended seminary. I don't have formal theological training or any degrees from prestigious institutions. I didn't spend years in classrooms filled with theological textbooks—not that I have anything against that—but it wasn't the path the Lord led me down.

Instead, my lessons came through the fire. My classroom was the wilderness. It was the valleys and mountain tops that Jesus walked, and the desert where He was tempted. It was the sacred ground that the Bible speaks of. My training ground was the quiet places where God met me—the hills of Kentucky, the dusty roads of Israel, and the storms I didn't think I'd survive. That's where I learned to hear His voice and trust His Word.

I don't have letters behind my name. I don't speak with polished words or flowery phrases. I speak plainly—sometimes even bluntly. But I've come to realize that what matters most is not the eloquence of the vessel, but the presence of the One who fills His willing vessels with power and purpose.

And yet, the question still echoed in my heart: *"Who am I?"*

Moses asked the same thing. *"Who am I, that I should go unto Pharaoh?"*—Exodus 3:11.

God didn't list his qualifications. He simply replied, *"Certainly I will be with thee."*—Exodus 3:12.

That's the only credential that matters.

I've felt the weight of others' unbelief. I've spoken in places where faith was missing, and the atmosphere grew cold. There have been moments when I held back because I feared how people would respond. But the more I resisted, the heavier the conviction became. I wasn't running from people—I was running from the call.

And I knew it. It was like God telling me, "Write a book with the same faith that led you to walk with Me. Rely on that same faith and let Me deal with the heart of the reader."

This went on for a few years. God wouldn't quit. I waited, and He kept nudging. I asked for signs like Gideon. I reminded God that I couldn't write—and He heard me.

> *"Faithful is He that calleth you, who also will do it."*
> —1 Thessalonians 5:24

It was early—about 4 a.m. on September 13, 2023—when I found myself praying once again, seeking direction. I didn't expect anything dramatic. I was just listening.

Then I heard it—not audibly, but unmistakably in my spirit: "Write a book."

I hesitated. I had heard it before. But this time, He didn't stop there. He gave me a name: Martina.

Martina Lucas—my cousin. We grew up close in a tight-knit family. Our parents worked together. We shared meals, played games, and laughed during holidays. She was smart, steady, and strong in faith. Life took us down different paths, and we lost touch over the years. But that morning, I knew I was supposed to reach out.

Later that day, I mentioned it to her sister, Cindy, not even knowing how to contact Martina. Cindy smiled and said, "She'll be in town tomorrow."

God's timing never ceases to amaze me.

Sure enough, the next day I received a text from Martina:

"I hear I'm helping you write your Faith Journeys in Israel book! How exciting!!! You tell me your stories, and I will start writing them down."

And that's how it began. I told her my stories, and she began to write them down. She got me started in the right direction.

Though life brought new responsibilities and paths, and I eventually continued writing on my own, she helped in those beginning steps—and it was a blessing I won't forget. This story—every word, every page—is my own testimony of what the Lord has done. But I honor those He sent to help me get started, like my cousin, Martina.

I remember wondering if we should leave out some of the more "unbelievable" parts—the supernatural encounters, the divine instructions, the moments that only faith can explain. But Martina looked me in the eye and said, "If this is God's book, then everything He's done belongs in it."

She was right.

Eventually, the writing became mine alone. But the foundation had been laid. And in His perfect timing, the Lord stirred my soul once more—not only to finish this book, but also to begin preparing another one. The call had never left.

Writing this book is not something I ever dreamed of doing. I didn't choose this—I surrendered to it. And now I understand: this book is my altar.

It's my Ebenezer stone—a declaration that says, *"Hitherto hath the Lord helped us"*—1 Samuel 7:12.

It's not just a collection of stories; it's a testimony. It's not about me—it's about the One who rescued me, shaped me, called me, and walked with me through it all. Every word is offered to bring Him glory. Every page is a witness to His presence and His power.

"I am the Lord thy God, the Holy One of Israel, thy Saviour"
—Isaiah 43:3.

If you're searching for something real… if you're wondering if God still speaks—I'm here to tell you: He does. And He's still calling. If you listen closely, you will hear Him whisper… ***"Come."***

Reflection

Stones have always mattered to God—not just as objects, but as witnesses. From the moment Abraham built altars to the stones that Jesus wept upon in Gethsemane, God has used them to mark holy ground. In your own life, the places where God met you—those are your stones. This book is mine. What are yours? Look back, remember, and thank Him. He was there.

Scripture

"What mean ye by these stones?"
—Joshua 4:6.

"Ye also, as lively stones, are built up a spiritual house…"
—1 Peter 2:5.

Prayer

Father, thank You for the sacred stones You've laid throughout my life—each one a reminder of Your presence, Your guidance, and Your grace. Help me to never forget where You've brought me from. May this book serve as an altar of remembrance, a testimony that points to Your faithfulness. And for those who read it, I pray they'll recognize the stones in their own lives—moments where You spoke, saved, and sent them forward. Let every word bring glory to Jesus Christ, the Chief Cornerstone. In His name I pray, Amen.

CHAPTER 2

Before Israel: A Journey to Faith

Before I tell you about my trips to Israel and the unforgettable moments walking where Jesus walked, I want to first share how I came to know Him—not just in history, but personally, as my Lord and Savior.

My journey to Jesus began at birth. When I was born, my grandfather—Minister Bob Hasty, whom we lovingly called "Pappy"—held me in his arms and prayed over me.

Pappy Hasty: A Pastor for Pastors

My grandfather, Bob Hasty, was more than just a local minister. Many who knew him said he was a pastor to pastors, a spiritual father, a man deeply connected to the voice of the Lord. But he didn't start that way.

Before he was ever known for preaching under the anointing of the Holy Spirit, he worked as a foreman at Kentucky Utilities in London, Kentucky, back in the 1960s. He was hardworking and respected—but like many men of that era, he also wrestled with his own demons. My Pappy liked to drink. In fact, he was well on his way to becoming an alcoholic.

6

He was a man searching for happiness in a bottle, but never finding it.

> *"There is a way which seemeth right unto a man, but the end thereof are the ways of death."*
> —Proverbs 14:12

One evening, after another night of drinking, he found himself walking alone through the woods—stumbling, perhaps, but not alone. That night, something happened that would change his life forever. He saw a vision: a man without a head.

To anyone else, it might sound strange. But to Pappy, that vision pierced his soul. It represented disconnection from God—the result of sin and a life lived apart from truth. It was a picture of a man without direction, without wisdom, and without life—a man spiritually dead.

> *"The fear of the Lord is the beginning of wisdom: and the knowledge of the holy is understanding"*
> —Proverbs 9:10.

> *"Having the understanding darkened, being alienated from the life of God through the ignorance that is in them..."*
> —Ephesians 4:18.

Terrified and convicted, he ran through the woods until he reached the nearest church house. He burst through the doors and headed straight to the altar. Yes, he was still drunk. Yes, the smell of alcohol was on him. But he fell to his knees and cried out to the Lord.

According to those who witnessed it, he rose from that altar a new man. The smell of alcohol was gone. His mind was sound. His spirit was awakened.

"Therefore if any man be in Christ, he is a new creature: old things are passed away; behold, all things are become new"
—2 Corinthians 5:17.

And what amazed the people in that church even more—he began to preach that very moment. The transformation was immediate, radical, and undeniable. He never stopped preaching for the rest of his life.

The Heart of a Shepherd

Pappy became a man led by the Holy Spirit—not just in his sermons, but in everyday life. Often, the Lord would tell him—clearly and specifically—who needed food, or shoes, or help for their children. After working long hours at Kentucky Utilities, he'd come home and tell my grandmother to get ready: "We need to go to the store."

He would buy exactly what the Lord had told him was needed, then personally deliver it to the families. My grandmother later told me how people would break down in tears and ask, "How did you know?"

His answer was always the same: "God told me."

"He that hath pity upon the poor lendeth unto the Lord; and that which he hath given will He pay him again"
—Proverbs 19:17.

"But whoso hath this world's good, and seeth his brother have need, and shutteth up his bowels of compassion from him, how dwelleth the love of God in him?"
—1 John 3:17.

Even on the job, people recognized him as a man of God. They would walk out to the roadside or across the fields where he worked, asking for prayer. He never turned them away.

The Atheist in the Field

One particular moment stands out in our family's legacy. A woman once approached him in a field and begged him to come pray for her husband, who had been sent home by the doctors to die. They said there was nothing more that could be done.

But Pappy knew the man was an atheist.

So he told her plainly: "No. Your husband doesn't believe in God, and I won't force myself into his home. Go back and ask if he's willing for me to come."

She ran back to her house and, by God's grace, convinced her husband to allow Pappy to come. So, she returned, breathless, and Pappy went with her.

He stood by the man's bedside and gently said something like, "I hear the doctors have done all they can for you. Now let me tell you about a man. His name is Jesus."

> "Neither is there salvation in any other: for there is none other name under heaven given among men, whereby we must be saved"
>
> —Acts 4:12.

Before he prayed, he looked the man in the eye and asked, "Do you now believe?" With a weak voice, the dying man said, "Yes."

The next day, while Pappy and his crew were back in the field working, the same woman came running again. She shouted, "Brother Hasty! You've got to come see my husband!"

When Pappy walked into the house, the man—who had been bedridden and dying the day before—was sitting at the table, eating!

He jumped up, ran to my grandfather, and fell to his knees, giving Pappy all the credit and praise. But my grandfather quickly corrected him—kicking him lightly and saying:

"Get up! I'm just a man. I didn't heal you—God did!"

"I am the Lord that healeth thee"

—Exodus 15:26.

"Not unto us, O Lord, not unto us, but unto thy name give glory..."

—Psalm 115:1.

A Legacy of Prayer

So yes—I believe with every fiber of my being that when Pappy Hasty held me in his arms as a baby and prayed that I would one day know and serve Jesus, that prayer took root. I believe it followed me all the days of my life. And I don't believe it was just his prayer.

It was the prayers of my mother, my grandmothers, and many others who quietly stood in the gap for me when I didn't even know I needed it.

"And all thy children shall be taught of the Lord; and great shall be the peace of thy children"

—Isaiah 54:13.

"The seed of the righteous shall be delivered"

—Proverbs 11:21b.

Their prayers were like a spiritual covering—a shield before I knew I was in battle.

Pappy's life reminds me that God can take even the most broken man and turn him into a vessel of mercy, healing, and truth. His story isn't just part of my past—it's the reason I know what it looks like when a man is completely surrendered to Jesus.

And because of that, I stand here today—not just as his grandson, but as a living testimony of what prayer can do across generations.

"The effectual fervent prayer of a righteous man availeth much"
—James 5:16.

"But the mercy of the Lord is from everlasting to everlasting upon them that fear him, and his righteousness unto children's children"
—Psalm 103:17.

Carried By Faith

At just 15 months old, I became dangerously ill. I already suffered from severe asthma, but something else had taken hold of me. My mom took me to our small-town hospital in Mt. Vernon and waited four long hours for help.

No one ever came.

Out of options, she left the hospital on foot, carrying me a block and a half to her parents' home. It was a bitterly cold day, with a frigid wind cutting through the air like a knife. My mother felt completely alone—desperate and afraid—unsure of what would happen to her only son. Fear pressed heavily on her chest, and every step felt like a weight she could barely carry. But even in the midst of her uncertainty, she held on to one unshakable truth: she had parents who knew how to pray.

The situation was taking an emotional toll not just on her, but also on my father. The weight of worry settled like a cloud over our entire family. Questions filled the silence: Would I make it? Would this be goodbye?

But even as fear crept in, faith rose up. Pappy took one look at me and said, "Dr. McCloud in Somerset is the best baby doctor around. I'm taking this baby to him."

Dr. McCloud feared the worst—leukemia—and admitted me immediately. I needed a blood transfusion. They took all they could from my dad, but it wasn't enough. Then the hospital asked a Black

11

woman—someone completely unknown to our family—if she would be willing to donate blood.

The Woman Who Gave Life

This was 1965. Racial tensions in America were high—a time when division, suspicion, and injustice were rampant. But none of that mattered to the woman who lay in that hospital room right down the hallway. Her heart was calm. Her spirit was tender. And her love for life—even a stranger's life—was greater than the boundaries the world tried to place between us.

She looked at the nurses and said with quiet courage,

"I've lived a good life. Take as much as you need if I can help save that baby's life."

She never asked about my skin color. She didn't ask about our background, our beliefs, or our family name. All she wanted to know was whether she could help. I thank God for her—for her selfless, Christlike love.

When I reflect on this moment, I see more than a kind act; I see in it the symbolism of Jesus—the One who gave His blood so that all of humanity could live. This woman was willing to give even unto death that I might live. Of course, the nurses would only take a portion of her blood. But Jesus—He gave it all.

"Greater love hath no man than this, that a man lay down his life for his friends"
—John 15:13.

"But God commendeth his love toward us, in that, while we were yet sinners, Christ died for us"
—Romans 5:8.

The Prayer That Found a Vein

While the medical team now had the blood they needed, the battle still wasn't over. The nurses tried everything, but they couldn't find a single vein that would accept the transfusion. They told my parents with somber faces that there was nothing more they could do. My veins were simply too small.

My father, doing all he could to help, gave as much blood as the doctors would allow. He sat up through the night watching over me, then went to work the next morning to keep the bills paid. But this was a fight that needed something more than what man could offer. It needed Heaven's intervention.

And that's when Pappy Hasty stepped in.

He didn't just visit the hospital—he stayed. All night long, he prayed at my bedside, lifting up his voice to the only One who could make a way where there was no way. And when the morning came, full of faith, he called the doctor and the nurse back into the room.

"Try again," he said.

The doctor and nurse looked at one another, unsure. They had already tried—more than once. But something about Pappy's voice carried weight. It wasn't just the voice of a concerned grandfather—it was the voice of faith.

So, they agreed.

One more time, they attempted the procedure. They searched for a vein... and this time, they found one.

What had seemed impossible just hours before—after every effort had failed—suddenly became possible. Not because of a new technique or advanced medicine, but because of the power of prayer. God had intervened.

> "Jesus beheld them, and said unto them, 'With men this is impossible; but with God all things are possible'"
> —Matthew 19:26.

13

"The effectual fervent prayer of a righteous man availeth much"

—James 5:16b.

I truly believe that if Pappy hadn't stayed and prayed through the night, I wouldn't have been here today. That moment wasn't just about a medical miracle—it was a spiritual one. It was the beginning of God's fingerprint on my life, showing me from the very start that He had a purpose for me. That His hand was upon me. That I had been spared for a reason.

And although I was too young to remember it, the story has been told and retold in my family—not as a tale of tragedy averted, but as a testimony of God's mercy.

That hospital room became holy ground—a place where Heaven touched earth, where a grandfather's prayer moved mountains, and where God said, "This one's mine."

"Before I formed thee in the belly I knew thee; and before thou camest forth out of the womb I sanctified thee..."
—Jeremiah 1:5.

"I shall not die, but live, and declare the works of the Lord"
—Psalm 118:17.

Sometime later, I spent a month in the hospital battling pneumonia under an isolation tent. My Aunt Ercel later told me it was one of the scariest times our family had ever faced. They didn't know if I would live or die.

Once again, God spared my life—for a purpose.

A Father's Trust and a Heavenly Reflection

As a boy, I had the freedom to roam our small town. My dad gave me one rule:

"I'm going to trust you until you prove I can't."

I never wanted to break that trust.

Looking back, this was instrumental in my life. I grew up never wanting to break that bond between me and my dad. The trust my father extended to me was more than permission—it was a relationship. It was a quiet understanding between father and son. I could talk to him about anything. That trust built a bridge between us that nothing else could.

But not everyone welcomed that closeness.

There were always a few people who tried to come between me and my father. Some would attempt to undermine our relationship, trying to cast doubt or stir division. Others would openly put me down in front of him while exalting themselves. But it never worked.

Dad saw through it all.

One day, after one of those moments, it was just me and him— alone together. I'll never forget what he said. He looked me square in the eye and said:

"Jeff, I don't know why people say and do those things... but you are my only son, and there is no one else who can ever change that."

That simple statement stuck with me. It was more than reassurance— it was identity, belonging, and unshakable love.

"This is my beloved Son, in whom I am well pleased"
—Matthew 3:17.

"The father of the righteous shall greatly rejoice: and he that begetteth a wise child shall have joy of him"
—Proverbs 23:24.

15

Now that my father has gone on to be with the Lord, I treasure that relationship even more. And as I reflect on it today, I see in it a powerful picture of my relationship with my Heavenly Father. My earthly father gave me a glimpse of what it means to be chosen, seen, and trusted.

But God—He desires even more for me. Now I lean fully on Him, trusting Him to meet every need.

> *"But my God shall supply all your need according to his riches in glory by Christ Jesus"*
> —Philippians 4:19.

The Trust That Gave Me Freedom

From our home on Shirley Street, I'd walk past Carter's Food Market and the courthouse, then down Main Street to Richmond Street, and finally to the elementary school playground.

That playground was more than just a place to swing and climb. It became a sacred space—a place where I first felt the Lord stirring something deep inside of me. I would cross that dusty field, and even though I couldn't explain it at the time, I knew—God was calling me.

Not to a career.
Not to a platform.
But to Himself.

> *"And a child shall lead them"*
> —Isaiah 11:6.

> *"Before I formed thee in the belly I knew thee... I ordained thee a prophet unto the nations"*
> —Jeremiah 1:5.

Standing My Ground

But not everyone welcomed me. Some bullies made it known they didn't want me around. They told me to take the long way to the ball field—to avoid their corner of the playground. But I never gave in.

I knew what was waiting, but I walked straight toward them anyway. Every time. They'd twist my arm in front of their older brother, who usually sat perched on the rock wall by the school. He never joined in. In fact, he just watched.

Eventually, after enduring enough bruises and "arm twists," I decided I'd climb up on the wall and sit beside him. Something unexpected happened—we became friends. While his younger brothers bullied just about everyone they could, he and I would sit and talk.

The next time I made that familiar walk to the field, the older brother saw me coming. This time, he stood up for me.

"Lay off Jeff," he said.

That was it. No more punches. No more harassment. Just like that, the attacks stopped.

"When a man's ways please the Lord, he maketh even his enemies to be at peace with him"
—Proverbs 16:7.

"The Lord is on my side; I will not fear: what can man do unto me?"
—Psalm 118:6.

Looking back now, I see it clearly—God was teaching me to stand my ground early. He was shaping something inside of me: perseverance, courage, and the ability to face conflict without running. He was showing me that when I walk with Him, I never walk alone.

I didn't give in.
I prayed.

I stood my ground.
God had my back.

"Blessed are ye, when men shall revile you, and persecute you, and shall say all manner of evil against you falsely, for my sake. Rejoice, and be exceeding glad: for great is your reward in heaven..."

—Matthew 5:11–12.

Just like that, God heard my prayers and softened the heart of the older brother. It may have seemed like a small victory at the time, but now I see it clearly—God was already shaping me, teaching me the power of prayer through childlike faith, simple obedience, and quiet trust in Him.

The Sound of the Gospel Through the Windows

Prayer came early in my life. I was raised in a church that believed in prayer—not just as a ritual, but as a living connection with a living God. And I believed in prayer because of the unwavering faith I saw in Pappy Hasty. Many Sundays, I'd sit on his knee while he bounced me up and down to the rhythm of a gospel song, slapping his other leg as he sang with joy.

It was something to hear him preach. People came from all over just to listen. Often, the church would be so full that folks had to stand outside. The leaders would raise the windows so they could still hear the Word going forth.

I remember one particular Sunday when a church leader approached my grandfather and said, "Brother Hasty, there are some men outside drinking. Do you want me to ask them to leave?"

Without hesitation, Pappy replied,

"Absolutely not. Raise up the windows—and I'll preach loud!"

He wasn't afraid of where those men were or what they were doing. He had been there himself once. He knew the power of grace. He knew the sound of chains breaking. And he knew that the same God who met him in the woods could meet them right there outside the church windows.

> *"Thou compassest my path and my lying down, and art acquainted with all my ways"*
> —Psalm 139:3.

Buried with Christ, Raised a New Man

As I grew older, I began to understand something profound—I could do nothing without Jesus in my life. Nothing of value. Nothing that lasted. So, I've often found myself going back to the Lord in prayer, saying:

"Lord, give me back that childlike faith. That early obedience. That deep trust I had in You when I didn't try to figure everything out—I just followed You."

And you know what? He honors that prayer. Because He knows that the ones who walk the farthest in faith are often those who first learned to walk in childlike dependence on Him.

Although I believed in Jesus from my childhood, at 16 years old, I publicly accepted Jesus as my Savior and was baptized in Brodhead Creek. It was one of the most important days of my life.

But just as my Uncle Henry and Aunt Margaret were about to pull into the field for the baptism, they were rear-ended.

"I knew I shouldn't have done this," I muttered, discouraged.

But Aunt Margaret wasn't having it.

"Don't you worry a bit about that! It's just a car that can be fixed. That old devil ain't gonna ruin your day!"

She was right.

It was a warm summer day, and I was filled with joy and anticipation. The day of my baptism had finally come. I had waited for this moment—not just to go into the water, but to publicly declare that I belonged to Jesus.

The man who baptized me was my great uncle, Pastor Charles Shivel, though I simply called him "Uncle." He was more than just family—he was my spiritual shepherd, my friend, and a wise advisor for many years. On that day, I remember looking into his face—he was almost as excited as I was.

Before we stepped into the water, Uncle Charles gave me a word of warning wrapped in love. He said:

"Our adversary will do everything in his power to pull you away from Christ, just like that wreck that tried to distract you today. But no matter what happens—keep your eyes on Jesus."

Then we waded out into the creek together. I stood beside him, the water swirling around us, and he began to speak to the crowd gathered on the bank. With strength in his voice and joy in his spirit, he said:

"As Jeff goes down into the water, it signifies that the old Jeff has died. And as he comes up out of the water, with the water falling from his body, it symbolizes the washing away of sins. As he stands, it represents Jeff as a new man—a new man in Christ!"

That moment still lives in my heart.

> *"Then Peter said unto them, 'Repent, and be baptized every one of you in the name of Jesus Christ for the remission of sins, and ye shall receive the gift of the Holy Ghost'"*
> —Acts 2:38.

I remember wishing so deeply that Pappy Hasty could have been there that day. He had gone to be with the Lord when I was just five years old. But in many ways, I believe God had handpicked Uncle Charles to stand in his place—to carry the baton, not only as a pastor, but as a man of God who would speak truth into my life for years to come.

Uncle Charles was more than a minister—he was a spiritual father. The kind of man who didn't just preach the gospel—he lived it.

That day, as the sun warmed the waters and the Spirit warmed my soul, I went down into that creek in faith—and rose in newness of life. Jesus had saved me. And there was no turning back.

"Therefore if any man be in Christ, he is a new creature: old things are passed away; behold, all things are become new"
—2 Corinthians 5:17.

Reflection

Some testimonies begin with a moment of radical conversion. Mine began with the prayers of a grandfather and the faith of a family who knew how to touch Heaven. From the very start, God's hand was upon my life—even when I didn't recognize it, even when others had given up. Through sickness, storms, playground trials, and spiritual awakenings, God was shaping a heart that would one day walk with Him. He used fathers and forefathers, faith and fire, to form the foundation of who I am today. The truth is, we never walk alone. When we look back through the pages of our lives, we find the fingerprints of a God who writes redemption into every line. This chapter is not just about my past—it's about God's persistent love that pursues generation after generation. It's about the power of prayer that never stops echoing. It's about the mercy that still reaches, still heals, still saves.

Scripture

"I will pour my spirit upon thy seed, and my blessing upon thine offspring"
—Isaiah 44:3.

Prayer

Father, thank You for the prayers of those who came before me. Thank You for the ones who stood in the gap, even when I didn't know I needed intercession. Thank You for sparing my life time and time again—not just for survival, but for purpose. You've been faithful from the beginning, and I see now that Your hand has never left me. Lord, help me to carry this legacy forward. Help me to be the one who prays, the one who stands, the one who believes even when the situation looks impossible. Teach me to trust You like a child again. Let every testimony in my life point to You. And may Your name be glorified from generation to generation.

In Jesus' name, Amen.

CHAPTER 3

The Fall and the Voice

During high school, I had dreams of becoming an electrical engineer. That wasn't just some passing idea—I had actually been working with a local electrician during the summer months since I was in fourth grade. Yes, fourth grade. I fell in love with the process of wiring homes, troubleshooting circuits, and learning how things worked. I even received a vocational school award for electrical wiring—something I was proud of.

Alongside that, I held down jobs at several restaurants as a busboy and dishwasher, including one owned by my Uncle Glen. It was during those long shifts at his restaurant that he drilled a principle into me that would shape the rest of my life: **"attention to detail."** At the time, I thought he was being too hard on me, but years later, I realized he was instilling a mindset that would become a foundational asset—especially in business.

At that time, I was old enough to drive, and I was making what I thought was good money. I bought my first car and worked every job I could find just to make more money. That was my rhythm all through high school—work, earn, build.

23

The Drift

But my life changed after I graduated. That childlike faith I had known as a boy—so pure, so sure—began to fade. I didn't notice it at first. It was subtle. Like a boat slowly drifting from the shoreline—not because of any great storm, but because it stopped being anchored.

I turned inward—toward "self." I began to believe the lie that I had to carve my own way, build my own kingdom, create my own success. I told myself that college was a waste of time. *"I don't need it,"* I thought. *"I've got enough drive, enough smarts. I'll make it on my own."*

And for a while—it looked like I was right.

Money started to come in. Opportunities showed up. People looked at me like I had it all figured out. I was proud of my independence, convinced that I had found a shortcut to the life others were still trying to reach.

But success without God is a house built on sand. It might look impressive for a season, but the foundation is shallow—and the cracks begin to show.

Looking back now, I can still hear the words my Uncle Charles spoke over me the day I was baptized. I was just a teenager, just before he took me into the water, he pulled me close and whispered a warning that now feels almost prophetic:

"Our adversary will do everything in his power to pull you away from Christ. Just like that wreck that tried to distract you today. But no matter what happens—keep your eyes on Jesus."

That wreck.

I wish I had remembered those words sooner.

Because over the next few years, I became that wreck. Not on the outside—no one could see it. But on the inside, I was all twisted up. Pride, anger, selfish ambition, and hidden pain were slowly eating away at the foundation of my life.

The truth is, I didn't drift because God failed me. I drifted because I stopped listening. I let the applause of man drown out the still, small voice of the Spirit. I let the rush of opportunity replace the discipline of devotion. I traded intimacy with God for independence of self.

But Jesus never stopped calling me back.

Even in my rebellion, He pursued me. Even when I silenced His voice, He never left me. That seed of childlike faith—planted deep in my heart by the Spirit—never died. It just went dormant for a while. And in His mercy, God began to stir it again.

That stirring came through hardship. Through nights I couldn't sleep. Through failed plans and closed doors. Through a growing sense that all my "success" was hollow. I had built a life, but it was empty of the one thing that mattered—*Him.*

It turns out Uncle Charles was right. The adversary did try to pull me away from Christ. And in some ways, he succeeded—for a time. But the greater truth is this:

Jesus never let go of me.

And just as surely as I had drifted, the Lord—so full of mercy— began calling me home. Not with shame. Not with condemnation. But with that same voice I'd known as a boy. That still, familiar voice that walked with me to the ball field. The voice that had never changed.

I'm still learning how to fix my eyes on Jesus. Still learning what it means to walk by faith, not by sight. But one thing I know: every detour, every fall, every failure has only deepened my dependence on Him.

And the voice of Uncle Charles still echoes in my soul:

"Keep your eyes on Jesus."

Reflection

Drifting from God doesn't always happen in a storm—it often starts in silence. A slow fade. A shift of focus. One moment you're anchored in faith, and the next, you're chasing applause, wealth, or independence. But even when we drift, God remains near. His voice doesn't change,

25

and His call doesn't stop. He lovingly steers us through closed doors, sleepless nights, and the ache of emptiness. Like a lighthouse for a ship lost at sea, His voice keeps shining—reminding us who we really are and where home truly is. When we turn from the lighthouse, we can never see the light. It's when we finally turn back, we see the Light and discover He never stopped calling our name. He was always there!

Scripture

"'Return, ye backsliding children,' saith the Lord; 'for I am married unto you...'"

—Jeremiah 3:14.

"My sheep hear my voice, and I know them, and they follow me."

—John 10:27.

Prayer

Gracious Heavenly Father, thank You for never giving up on me—even when I turned my back on You. Forgive me for the times I chased my own way instead of walking in Yours. Thank You for the still, small voice that kept calling me back, even when I wasn't listening. Plant my feet firmly on the foundation of Christ. Let my life be built not by my own hands, but by Your Word, Your will, and Your Spirit. May I never forget the voice that called me home.

In Jesus' name, Amen.

CHAPTER 4

The Kingdom and the Collapse

Straight out of high school, I landed a job as an assistant manager at Convenient Food Mart in Mt. Vernon. Before long, I was helping at other locations in Brodhead and Corbin. Within a year, I was promoted to manager at the Mt. Vernon store—and then, I purchased the Franchise.

I've never been afraid of hard work. In fact, I prided myself on it. I was a self-proclaimed workaholic, and I wore it like a badge of honor. I started seeing my business as a kingdom—*my* kingdom. One that I could build brick by brick, dollar by dollar.

I quickly paid $100,000 down on my bank note. Then I purchased the property next to the store and built a self-service car wash. The following year, I bought out my competitor's car wash in town. I acquired other ventures. I lived in a beautiful home in a nice subdivision. I bought a Porsche, a BMW, and a couple of other vehicles just for show.

I had the need for speed!

Life was good—at least, from the outside looking in.

I was rubbing shoulders with company presidents, CEOs, and a few notable names. I received invitations to exclusive business events and conferences. I had become the definition of "young and successful" at only 21 years old.

And I loved to tell people how great I was and everything I had built with my own hands.

But not once did I give God credit.
Not once.
That childlike faith was long gone.
I wasn't the man I was supposed to be.
But God knew it.
And everything was about to change.

> *Pride goeth before destruction, and an haughty spirit before a fall*
>
> —Proverbs 16:18.

> *Lest when thou hast eaten and art full, and hast built goodly houses... then thine heart be lifted up, and thou forget the Lord thy God*
>
> —Deuteronomy 8:12–14.

The Voice in the Yard

A few years later, I decided to sit down and tally up my net worth. The number surprised even me.

"Wow," I said aloud.

"I knew I could do it."

I was proud—*too* proud.

That day, I decided to take a break. I came home, looked around at the fruit of my labor—my brick house, the luxury cars, the steady stream of income—and I hopped on my mower to cut the grass.

It was a perfect day. The air was just right—not too hot, not too cold. The smell of fresh-cut grass filled my lungs. As I rode across the yard, I felt a deep satisfaction of *self.*

"This is all mine."

"I've made it."

"What's next?"

"What am I going to buy next?"

And then, it happened.

Out of nowhere, I heard a Voice:

"I will take everything from you, even as if overnight. You shall have only the clothes on your back."

I froze.

The mower still hummed beneath me, but my mind was spinning.

Where did that come from?

Was that my imagination?

I shook it off.

Whatever.

I kept mowing.

But I had just heard the voice of God—and I ignored it.

I even smirked to myself.

"I'm the greatest. I'm the one who made this life. I hold my future in my hands."

Still, the Voice echoed in my spirit. I couldn't shake it.

> *"And thine ears shall hear a word behind thee, saying, This is the way, walk ye in it..."*
> —Isaiah 30:21.

The Fall

Once I had "made it," I began to pull back. I started hiring people to run the day-to-day operation of my businesses. I traveled. Bought more toys. Took life easy. And then—seven months later—it all came crashing down. Like a boulder rolling downhill, nothing could stop the collapse.

- My businesses began to fail.
- My marriage began to unravel.
- My five-year-old son, Jeffrey, was caught in the middle—passed between two homes.

29

In my brokenness, I began to blame Lisa—my wife at the time—for everything that had gone wrong. But the truth is, Lisa was a good wife and an incredible mother to our son, Jeffrey. Our home was a place of peace, always clean, always welcoming. She created an environment of stability and love.

But I kept running from God, and that distance from Him is what ultimately drove a wedge between me and my wife. I couldn't see it then. My pride blinded me. But as I've grown older—and hopefully wiser—I can look back now and say with complete clarity:

I was wrong. I was foolish. And let me be very clear—**God did not cause my marriage to fail. I did.** I take full responsibility for the collapse of my marriage. It wasn't God's doing. It was mine.

> *"But he giveth more grace. Wherefore he saith, God resisteth the proud, but giveth grace unto the humble"*
> —James 4:6.

Regardless of all that was going on in my mind, I could not quench the thought of the Voice.

Still, I wouldn't listen. I hardened my heart. I raged at God. If He didn't care, then I wouldn't either.

> *"Be not deceived; God is not mocked: for whatsoever a man soweth, that shall he also reap"*
> —Galatians 6:7.

> *"For whom the Lord loveth he chasteneth, and scourgeth every son whom he receiveth"*
> —Hebrews 12:6.

Running from God

In my anger and brokenness, I just wanted to disappear—to get away from everyone and everything. The friends I once trusted had vanished. Even some of my own family turned their backs on me. I felt completely abandoned. Honestly, I couldn't think of a single person who truly cared—or at least, that's how it seemed.

To make matters worse, the relationship with my father had suffered deeply because of my failed marriage. There was tension where there used to be trust. It all felt like too much.

I was angry. I was bitter. Especially at God. Why did He let this happen? Why didn't He stop it? I was alone. Truly broken. And for the first time, I realized—I couldn't fix myself.

> *"The Lord is nigh unto them that are of a broken heart;*
> *and saveth such as be of a contrite spirit"*
> —Psalm 34:18.

Reflection

Sometimes, God must allow the very kingdoms we build for ourselves to crumble before we'll acknowledge the King who reigns over all. Success, comfort, and pride can deceive us into thinking we are self-made—but the truth is, every breath we breathe is a gift from God. When we forget the Giver, He may lovingly strip away the gifts—not to destroy us, but to restore us. The collapse isn't the end; it's often the beginning of a deeper call to repentance, humility, and grace. When we fall, He is there. When we lose it all, He offers us Himself.

Scripture:

"Charge them that are rich in this world, that they be not highminded, nor trust in uncertain riches, but in the living God, who giveth us richly all things to enjoy"
—1 Timothy 6:17.

"Humble yourselves therefore under the mighty hand of God, that he may exalt you in due time"
—1 Peter 5:6.

Prayer:

Father, thank You for loving me enough to correct me. Even when I ignored Your voice, You didn't stop speaking. Even when I built my own kingdom and took the glory for myself, You patiently waited, calling me back through grace and truth. Lord, forgive me for the pride that blinded me and the distance I created between us. Thank You for allowing what I built to fall, so that what You desire to build in me could begin. I surrender my heart, my future, and my plans to You now. Tear down anything in me that competes with Your Lordship, and help me to walk in humility and truth. May I never again forget that You are the One who gives and sustains all things. My life is Yours. In Jesus' name, Amen.

CHAPTER 5

Into the Army

I made a drastic decision: I enlisted in the United States Army. Even though enlisting meant being away from my son, I just had to get away. I was running. Running from failure. Running from pain. Running from God Himself.

But deep down, the hardest part of it all was saying goodbye to my son, Jeffrey. At that moment, something broke inside me. As I looked into his eyes, I knew I wasn't just walking away from a place—I was walking away from the most important relationship in my life.

As I left him behind, a part of me believed I would never come back. I didn't expect to survive.

And to be honest, I didn't think I deserved to.

I joined in March of 1992, shortly after the Gulf War. I wasn't there to serve—I was there to escape. The Army was supposed to be a hiding place from the storm inside me.

I volunteered for everything—daring God to follow through.

When I arrived at Boot Camp at Fort Knox, I didn't flinch. I actually looked forward to what was coming. I knew it was all a game to the barking drill sergeants—and I was ready to play.

I made a proclamation to God:

"My blood is on Your hands. The only way I'm going back to Mt. Vernon is in a body bag."

33

When I arrived at Fort Knox, I had nothing but the clothes on my back—just like the Voice had said.

Well, that and a small bag with cologne and a blow dryer, of all things.

Pride dies hard.

I placed the bag on my cot and arrogantly thought,

See, God? I have more than just the clothes on my back. You were wrong.

Then the Drill Sergeant walked in. He zeroed in on my bag. **"Dump it!"** I dumped it. Out came the cologne and the blow dryer.

He got in my face. Berated me. Made an example out of me in front of everyone. Then, to top it off, he confiscated everything.

And there I stood. Just like the Voice had said. With only the clothes on my back.

"But he giveth more grace. Wherefore he saith, God resisteth the proud, but giveth grace unto the humble"
—James 4:6.

"For whosoever exalteth himself shall be abased; and he that humbleth himself shall be exalted"
—Luke 14:11.

Breaking and Pursuing

Although I hadn't yet surrendered to God, something in me was breaking more with each passing day. I remember lying in my bunk at night, staring at the ceiling, wondering what would become of me.

Did I even have a future?

I was still angry—bitter toward God. I never stopped to examine what I had done wrong. In my pride, I still saw myself as "the greatest." I believed that God had failed me... not the other way around.

But now, looking back with clearer eyes, I see it: God was pursuing me, even while I was running from Him in a storm of rage. Even in my rebellion, He hadn't let go.

"If we believe not, yet he abideth faithful: he cannot deny himself"
—2 Timothy 2:13.

"The Lord is nigh unto them that are of a broken heart..."
—Psalm 34:18.

Helicopter Mechanic Training – Fort Eustis, Virginia

After boot camp, I was assigned to Fort Eustis, Virginia, for helicopter mechanic training. But I still wasn't done fighting God.

One day, I started feeling sick and running a fever. I refused to tell anyone. I still had a death wish. I didn't care if I lived or died.

Eventually, it caught up to me. One morning, when I didn't report to roll call, the Senior Drill Sergeant found me unconscious in the top bunk of my cot. He rushed me to the hospital, where they discovered I had a 105-degree fever. I was hospitalized for about four days, but the cause of the illness was never identified.

Because of the days I'd missed, my training schedule was now behind. The officers considered "recycling" me—holding me back to join the next class. But the Senior Drill Sergeant stepped in and said, **"No. He can make it up."**

And I did—graduating at the top of my class.

My Jonah Moment

I was like Jonah in the Bible. Stubborn. Reluctant. Running from the very call that God had placed on my life. Jonah didn't want to go

35

where God told him to go, so the Lord sent a whale—not as punishment, but as redirection. A divine intervention wrapped in discipline. That whale didn't just swallow Jonah; it swallowed his pride, his fear, and his rebellion. And after three days in the belly of that whale, Jonah was spit out—humbled, changed, and ready to obey.

In many ways, I was living out my own version of that story.

I didn't board a ship to Tarshish, but I did chart my own course, determined to go my own way. I made plans without prayer. I chased success instead of surrender. And every time I thought I was getting ahead, life would cave in around me. Doors would shut. Circumstances would spin. People would disappoint. What I thought was bad luck was really the mercy of God—stepping in, surrounding me, not letting me drift too far from His will.

> *"Thou hast beset me behind and before, and laid thine hand upon me"*
>
> —Psalm 139:5.

I couldn't escape Him, no matter how hard I tried.

> *Whither shall I go from thy spirit? Or whither shall I flee from thy presence? If I ascend up into heaven, thou art there: if I make my bed in hell, behold, thou art there. If I take the wings of the morning, and dwell in the uttermost parts of the sea; even there shall thy hand lead me, and thy right hand shall hold me*
>
> —Psalm 139:7–10.

The more I ran, the more He stepped in. And it wasn't always gentle. Sometimes it felt like everything I touched turned to dust. But looking back now, I see it clearly: God was not trying to ruin me. **He was rescuing me.**

Just like Jonah, I had to be broken in order to be rebuilt. My detours became divine classrooms. My pain became preparation. God was shaping me—chipping away at my stubborn will, softening my heart, and aligning my steps with His perfect plan.

It wasn't a whale that got my attention. It was a series of moments—a dream, a voice, a closed door, a divine appointment—that finally brought me to my knees. And that's when I realized: the safest place to be is not in the comfort of my own plans, but in the center of God's will. Even if it leads me into deep waters.

God had every reason to turn His face from me. I was angry, ungrateful, and bitter. Yet, He kept blessing me—not because I was good, but because He is. Even while I was wallowing in rebellion, He was already rebuilding me into the man He had called me to be.

I've received grace upon grace.

"And of his fulness have all we received, and grace for grace"
—John 1:16.

And even now, it still blows my mind.

Fort Campbell, Kentucky

My next assignment was Fort Campbell, Kentucky—a base that sits mostly in Tennessee but has a Kentucky mailing address. I was in the best shape of my life. I could run 12 to 15 miles with no problem. Every time I ran, I knew in my heart that it was God who had healed me.

We ran 30 to 35 miles a week in PT. I had been so built up physically and mentally that I could literally run circles around my company—and I did. I usually carried the guidon (a pole with a flag on it) and ran beside the Commander. But sometimes, I'd slip out of the formation and start running loops around it.

"Cromer, you need to run a marathon!"

At my Company Commander's request, I entered a half-marathon and finished strong—though I can't recall exactly what place I finished, I know it was near the top.

Going Home: Meeting My Future Wife

One of the best things about being stationed at Fort Campbell was being within driving distance of home. On my weekends off, I could visit Mt. Vernon and see Jeffrey. Those visits meant everything to me.

It was during one of those weekends in the fall of 1994 that I met the woman who would later become my wife. My parents were running a grocery store in Livingston at the time, in a building they rented from Bobby Wilson. While visiting them, I saw a tan-legged girl in white shorts walk into the store. My first thought was:

"Who is that gorgeous woman?" I soon found out she was Bobby's daughter. We didn't start dating then, but that was how we met.

The Barber's Chair

As time passed and the Lord began drawing my heart back to Him, I found myself making more and more frequent trips to Livingston. I can't fully explain why—it wasn't for anything specific at first. Maybe it was the quiet hills. Maybe it was the memories that lingered in the streets, the smell of woodsmoke in the air, or the familiar way the wind seemed to speak across the ridges. But something inside me felt drawn to that little town again.

And on many of those trips, I'd stop by Billy Medley's barbershop.

Billy was a local fixture. If you spent any time in Livingston, you knew him. His shop wasn't fancy—just a simple room with a barber chair, a mirror, and a Bible on the counter. There was usually an old radio playing softly in the background, tuned to gospel music or bluegrass. The place smelled of shaving cream, hair tonic, and the kind of comfort that can't be bottled.

But it wasn't just the haircuts that kept me coming back.

It was Billy.

Billy Medley had a way about him. He could talk about Jesus like He'd just walked out the door and was about to come back in for coffee.

There was nothing forced, nothing religious or rehearsed. No stage lights. No show. Just honest, humble faith wrapped in kindness.

"He's good, you know," Billy would say casually as he trimmed around my ears. **"He'll watch over you."**

And that was it. He never thumped a Bible. He never lectured me or asked what I'd been doing wrong. He just spoke truth in love—like Jesus Himself might do in a barbershop chair.

Something in me started to change.

At first, it was small. A soft tug. A whisper. But I couldn't deny that every time I sat in that chair, something in my heart felt lighter. I'd walk in carrying the weight of the world—and somehow leave with peace.

The Ministry of a Barber

Billy reminded me of who I used to be, before the world hardened my edges. His gentle words stirred memories of old church services in Livingston and Mt. Vernon, of tent meetings and wooden pews, of hymns sung with conviction and a childlike faith I thought I had lost forever.

My anger—which had once gripped my heart so tightly—began to fade. Slowly, God was softening me. Reminding me that He hadn't left. That He still wanted me. That there was still time.

And today—years later—I see how God was working even in those simple moments. He used a barber's chair to bring me closer to His presence.

Even more incredible, Billy's son, Jason Medley, and I are now good friends. Just like his dad, Jason followed the Lord—not just in life, but into the same calling. He's also a barber... and a pastor! Who would've guessed? Only God could write a story like that.

Jason cuts hair with one hand and ministers with the other. You'll hear about Jesus in his chair, too—same as it was with Billy. Maybe a little different in style, but the message hasn't changed.

Grace still flows from the barbershop.

So, if you ever find yourself passing through Livingston, Kentucky, and you need a haircut—or maybe just a moment of peace—stop by and see Jason Medley. He'll line up your hair and speak truth to your soul.

Because some chairs aren't just for trimming hair…

Some are altars. And some barbers carry more than clippers—they carry hope.

Reflection

There are moments in life when we run so far from God that we wonder if we could ever make it back. Yet, in every corner of this Chapter, we see a God who does not give up—who speaks through drill sergeants, softens hearts in barber chairs, and reaches into the storms we try to weather alone. This chapter reminds us that grace is not earned. It finds us in rebellion, redeems us in brokenness, and redefines our future. Even in our lowest moments, God is still writing a higher story.

Scripture

"The Lord upholdeth all that fall, and raiseth up all those that be bowed down"
—Psalm 145:14.

"He brought me up also out of an horrible pit, out of the miry clay, and set my feet upon a rock, and established my goings"
—Psalm 40:2.

"Where sin abounded, grace did much more abound"
—Romans 5:20.

Prayer

Lord, thank You for pursuing me even when I was running away. Thank You for the grace that met me in my brokenness, for the mercy that covered my pride, and for the still, small voice that never stopped calling. I surrender the failures of my past into Your hands and ask that You continue to lead me with Your truth and love. Restore what was lost, heal what was broken, and use my life for Your glory.

In Jesus' name, Amen.

CHAPTER 6

The Face That Brought Me Back

Something pretty cool happened—I studied real estate law in my spare time and became a licensed real estate agent in the State of Tennessee!

Why? It was something to do in my spare time! It became an ambition. I had been broken; now it was time to heal. Although I would never sell real estate in Tennessee—because I received orders to go to Germany—God was getting me ready for His future plans.

> "A man's heart deviseth his way: but the Lord directeth his steps"
>
> —Proverbs 16:9.

Once again, I thought I had a plan, but God had different plans for me. I didn't get to stay stateside much longer.

A Familiar Face

Something happened that I still can't fully explain—but I know it was more than coincidence. It was early morning, and I was walking out the door of the barracks, boots laced up, mind on the day ahead, when I came face to face with a man I had never met before.

42

He wore command with quiet confidence. His uniform was crisp, and the weight of his presence demanded respect. He didn't have to say a word—you just knew he was someone of authority.

He was my Sergeant Major.

But that's not what caught me off guard.

I froze for a moment, stunned. My eyes locked onto his face, and I couldn't help but stare. It was awkward—I knew better than to gawk at a senior-ranking non-commissioned officer—but I couldn't look away. My heart began to pound in my chest.

Something in his eyes... the shape of his face... even the way he stood—it all felt familiar.

He noticed, of course. His brow furrowed slightly, curious, maybe even a little annoyed, wondering why this young soldier was staring at him like he'd seen a ghost.

Finally, I broke the silence and said, "Excuse me, Sergeant Major, for staring... but you look so much like my grandfather. He died when I was five—but you sure do favor him."

We talked briefly—just a few words exchanged—but in those moments, he gave me his utmost attention. He wasn't distracted or hurried like so many leaders often are. He looked me in the eyes, and there was something steady, almost fatherly, about his presence.

When our conversation ended and he turned to go, I didn't move.

It wasn't out of confusion or duty—it was something deeper. A wave of emotion surged over me like a tide that had been rising quietly for years, finally crashing against the shore of my heart.

I felt five years old again.

Memories I hadn't visited in decades suddenly came alive with color and clarity—my grandfather's voice, his laugh, the smell of his hair tonic, the sound of his boots coming up the porch steps. I could see his silhouette in the doorway, and could almost feel his arms lifting me up again.

It was a divine reminder. A gift from God. A thread He had kept tied to my heart all these years, tugging it gently in just the right moment to remind me:

You are known. You are seen. You are still My child.

Tears didn't fall, but they welled up. Not of sadness—of thankfulness.

Because even in the middle of duty and discipline, God found me again.

I hadn't thought about my grandfather in a long time. Life had moved fast—military duties, personal struggles, spiritual ups and downs. But all at once, it was like God cracked open a window in my soul and let in a gust of memories I didn't know I still had.

One memory in particular came rushing back with clarity: the little boy who used to walk to the ball field all by himself. Not worried about who was in the way. Not afraid of being alone. Just walking by faith—believing that if he kept moving forward, he wasn't walking alone.

That boy hadn't disappeared. He'd just grown up. Gotten battle-worn. But God was calling him back. Back to simplicity. Back to trust. Back to walking by faith, not by sight.

Looking back now, I see that moment at the barracks for what it truly was: a divine reminder. That Sergeant Major wasn't just another face in uniform. He was a signpost. A gentle whisper from Heaven saying:

I see you. I know where you've come from. And I haven't forgotten who you are.

> *"And he shall turn the heart of the fathers to the children,*
> *and the heart of the children to their fathers..."*
> —Malachi 4:6a.

That moment not only played an important role in my life, but it also moved the heart of my Sergeant Major.

An Unspoken Prayer Answered

A couple of weeks later, I was called into his office. There wasn't any warning—no explanation—just a summons.

I sat down, unsure of what this was about, and tried to read his expression. After a moment of silence, he looked up and said, "I've heard that you don't want to go to Korea."

My heart dropped. How did he know that? I hadn't told anyone in leadership. Only a few of my closest friends knew.

I had spoken a prayer under my breath—quietly and earnestly—that God might open another door.

So, I sat up straight, composed myself, and answered the best I knew how: "Sergeant Major, I'll go wherever the Army sends me."

He nodded thoughtfully, then leaned in and said something I never expected to hear:

"Well, you've got a choice—Korea or Germany. I'll let you pick."

I had heard of others being handed orders—but never options. This was God answering an unspoken prayer. He had seen my heart, heard my silent petitions, and moved in a way only He could.

Without much hesitation, I chose Germany. He told me that once my official orders came through, I'd be granted a 30-day leave before deploying overseas.

That conversation would end up being the last time I ever spoke with him.

Reflection

Sometimes, all it takes is a familiar face to awaken what's been sleeping in our hearts. God doesn't always shout—He often whispers through memory, through kindness, through presence. When He does, it's not just a reminder—it's a rescue.

Scripture

"I will instruct thee and teach thee in the way which thou shalt go: I will guide thee with Mine eye"
—Psalm 32:8.

Prayer

Lord, thank You for never forgetting me. Even when life gets loud and I forget who I am, You remember. Thank You for using familiar faces and unexpected moments to speak to my heart. Bring me back to that place of trust and simple faith. In Jesus' name, Amen.

CHAPTER 7

Coming Home

One day, while we were working in the hangar, someone asked a group of us, "If you could meet any historical figure, who would it be?"

Without even thinking, I answered: "Jesus."

The guy shook his head. "No, somebody real."

"He is real!" I shot back.

"Okay, okay. Somebody famous—someone actually alive that you can see."

Without missing a beat, I said: "Roy Rogers."

Another guy perked up. "Oh! His museum is right down the road from where I live—in Apple Valley, California."

So that's where I decided to go during part of my 30-day leave. I had no idea that meeting Roy Rogers would be connected to one of the most important spiritual turning points in my life.

The Cowboy Who Shaped a Kid

Roy Rogers was one of my childhood heroes. I grew up glued to our black-and-white television, watching *The Roy Rogers Show* with wide eyes and a wild imagination. To me, Roy wasn't just a cowboy—he was *the* cowboy. Clean-cut, honorable, and always doing what was right, he stood for something good in a world that didn't always make sense.

As a little boy, I'd grab one of my mom's feather pillows, toss it onto the living room floor, and go to town wrestling it like it was a no-good outlaw. All the while, Roy would be galloping across the screen on Trigger, saving the day with a smile and a steady hand. He inspired me. He was a role model I looked up to—someone I wanted to be like.

A Divine Appointment

When I first arrived at the Roy Rogers Museum, it was late in the evening. The warm California sun had already started its descent, casting long shadows across the parking lot. As I stepped through the doors, a staff member kindly greeted me and said, "You just missed him. Roy's gone home for the day—but he will be back around 8 a.m."

I nodded, disappointed but determined. "I'll be back," I said.

And I was.

The next morning, I showed up a few minutes after the doors opened. By that time, a busload of eager fans had already arrived and were gathered at the front, buzzing with excitement. I stepped inside, looked down into a slightly sunken entry area—and there he was.

Roy Rogers himself.

Wearing his trademark cowboy hat and a kind smile, he looked like an older, wiser version of the man I used to watch on the black-and-white television. Time had added lines to his face, but the same noble presence remained. He was every bit the hero I had imagined—and more.

He stood patiently while the crowd filtered in, nodding and greeting folks as they passed. Then, for a brief moment, it was just the two of us in an open room.

I stepped forward.

"Mr. Rogers," I said, my voice laced with both excitement and respect, "you were my hero growing up. I used to watch your show all the time."

He smiled warmly. "Well, thank you, partner. That means a lot."

"I'd sit on the floor with a feather pillow and beat it like I was in a wild west brawl—pretending to be you."

He laughed. "A feather pillow, huh? That's one way to take down the bad guys."

We kept talking. The conversation flowed easily, like two old friends reconnecting. I told him I was from Kentucky.

His eyes lit up. "No kidding? My mama was from Kentucky."

Something about that connection made the conversation feel even more personal. I told him I was in the Army and had just received orders to deploy to Germany.

His expression changed. His posture straightened, and a flicker of emotion crossed his face. "I lost a son in Germany," he said quietly.

The joy in the room seemed to pause for a moment. His words hung heavy between us—sincere, heartfelt, and full of unspoken pain. I nodded respectfully, not knowing what to say. And maybe no words were needed. It was one of those moments when silence spoke volumes.

A Trusted Moment

By then, more busloads of visitors had arrived. Roy told me, "Make yourself at home until the bus crowds clear out. Then we'll talk again."

As I walked through the museum, I could see how much Roy had been blessed in his life. I learned about the boys' home he had founded. I saw the legacy he had built with the blessings of God.

Later, Roy shared with me that he had earned just $300 per TV episode. But he had wisely invested that money—and he had never sold the rights to his name. Then he said something that stuck with me:

"The more I gave, the more God blessed."

Give, and it shall be given unto you; good measure, pressed down, and shaken together, and running over, shall men

49

give into your bosom. For with the same measure that ye mete withal it shall be measured to you again.

—Luke 6:38

That one statement convicted me. I knew I was still running from God—but something was shifting. My heart was being stirred.

As we talked, Roy's son arrived and joined the conversation. He looked at me and said:

"Wow, you look more like my dad than I do!"

Before I left, Roy walked me out to my car. He told me he had plans to build a motel and restaurant next to the museum. Then he looked me in the eye and said:

"But I'd appreciate it if you don't say anything about that."

I never did say anything. Not then. Not until he told it publicly.

There are moments in life that feel almost sacred—not because they happen in a church or during some formal ceremony, but because of the trust they carry. What Roy Rogers shared with me that day was one of those moments.

He spoke with a tenderness that didn't need a microphone or a crowd. It wasn't part of any public statement, wasn't something said for applause or legacy. It was a father's grief—and a man's heart, cracked open just enough for someone else to see inside. And for reasons I can only attribute to the Lord, he chose to share it with me.

A Quiet Legacy

What struck me most about Roy Rogers was not the fame, the legend, or the cowboy hat. It was the way he carried himself—with grace, humility, and the same warmth he showed on screen. He had known deep sorrow, yet he never let it define him. Somehow, through it all, he held onto joy. Roy didn't just *play* a cowboy who trusted in God—he truly was a man who walked by faith.

Behind the silver screen smile stood a man of deep conviction. Roy Rogers was a Christian, and both he and his wife, Dale Evans, spoke openly about their relationship with Jesus Christ. Raised in a simple Baptist home in Ohio and Kentucky, Roy's faith was first nurtured in small country churches, where his mother's gentle influence planted seeds that would take root for a lifetime.

Hollywood fame never stole that foundation. Even surrounded by wealth and opportunity, Roy and Dale remained steadfast in their family-friendly, faith-centered values. Their testimony only deepened when tragedy struck. After the heartbreaking loss of their daughter Robin, Dale poured her grief into the book *Angel Unaware* (1953). It was not a story of despair, but of God's comfort and grace in the darkest valley. That little book rippled across America, bringing encouragement to countless Christian families who had walked through similar sorrows.

Together, Roy and Dale carried their faith far beyond the screen. They stood in pulpits and at crusades, including alongside Billy Graham—not as celebrities, but as humble witnesses to the saving power of Jesus Christ. As Roy grew older, he made it clear that his ultimate hope was not in his career but in his Savior. Dale once put it best: *"Roy wasn't just a cowboy star; he was a cowboy who loved Jesus."*

Before we parted ways, Roy did something I will never forget. He looked me in the eye, patted me on the back, and said with genuine kindness:

"Anytime you hear that I'm at the Grand Ole Opry, just come down and tell them, 'Jeff Cromer is here to see Roy Rogers—backstage.' They'll bring you on back."

I was floored. Roy Rogers himself had just invited me backstage at one of the most iconic stages in country music. It wasn't a casual offer—it was sincere, personal, and generous.

That gesture spoke more about his character than any fame or title ever could.

I smiled, nodded, and carried that moment in my heart. But life moved quickly. I never did get the chance to take him up on that invitation. Soon, I was off to Germany, called to serve my country, unaware of all that God would unfold in my life and faith in the years to come.

Sometimes I wonder what might have happened had I walked through those backstage doors. What more we might have shared. What wisdom Roy might have passed on. Yet even without that second conversation, I carry his words with me—the memory of his honesty, his sorrow, and his generosity.

And I carry the lesson that some of the greatest ministries don't happen in pulpits or stadiums. They happen in quiet corners, when one person decides to speak and another chooses to listen. That's what Roy did for me.

By God's grace, I pray I've carried that same spirit into every conversation since.

A Prophetic Confirmation

A few days later, I was back in the hangar at Fort Campbell. The Nashville News Network came on the radio with breaking news: Roy Rogers had just shared his plans to build a new motel and restaurant on museum property.

I chuckled to myself and told the guys, "I already knew about that. Roy Rogers told me."

Of course, nobody believed me. They didn't even know I had met him. That's okay. Even to this day, I usually keep it quiet when I meet famous people. I've always preferred real relationships over name-dropping. That's when you know you've got a true friend.

The Dream

In June of 1995, something happened that I'll never forget. I had a vivid, terrifying dream—so real that it still shakes me when I think about it. In the dream, I was being dragged down into Hell. I could feel and see the flames like a great furnace heated hotter than any fire I had ever seen. I heard the screams. I could feel the pull on my legs.

In the dream, I even screamed out loud—calling out to that one name: Jesus! "Jesus! Help me!"

That was the only name I knew that could save me. A name above all, both in Heaven and on Earth. He is Jesus.

When I finally woke up, I was at the very edge of my lower bunk. From the knees down, my legs were hanging off the bed like something—or someone—had been trying to pull me off.

I asked my roommate later if he had heard me talking in my sleep, but he told me he hadn't heard a thing.

I could never describe the feeling that I had except to say: All hope was gone. It was the end, and there was nothing anyone could do.

Growing up in church and being part of a Christian family who believed in Jesus—that's what saved me in my dream, because I knew a name that could deliver me before it was too late.

Jesus pulled me out of the fire.

"And others save with fear, pulling them out of the fire..."
—Jude 1:23a.

Coming Home

That following Sunday, I drove home from Fort Campbell and went to a local church. I couldn't wait for the pastor to finish preaching. I had a made-up mind. I was done running. I was ready to surrender.

I made my way to the altar. As I invited Jesus back into my life, asking for His forgiveness, I felt the love of God flood my heart like warm oil being poured over a wound. I came back to the child I had once been—the boy who loved Jesus with everything he had.

From that point forward, I went home for church every weekend that I could. And I started sharing my testimony with some of my fellow soldiers. I wasn't perfect, but something had changed.

The Lord had pulled me out of the pit—literally in my dream, and spiritually in real life. I had come home to more than Kentucky. I had come Home to Jesus.

Reflection

You can run from God—but you can't outrun His grace. He knows where to find you. And when you call on the name of Jesus, even from the edge of Hell, He answers. He doesn't just rescue you—He restores you.

Scripture

"Therefore if any man be in Christ, he is a new creature: old things are passed away; behold, all things are become new"
—2 Corinthians 5:17.

Prayer

Jesus, thank You for saving me. Thank You for meeting me in a place of fear and showing me that Your mercy has no limits. I surrender again—heart, soul, and future. Teach me to walk with You daily, and help me never forget the power of Your Name. Amen.

CHAPTER 8

The Word on the Mountain

In 1995, just before I left for Germany, I made one final trip back home. I didn't know it at the time, but that visit would mark a spiritual turning point. During those few quiet days at home, the Lord called me to do something unusual—something I never would have chosen on my own. He told me to go up to the top of a mountain at Mullins Station, a rugged piece of land nestled deep in the Kentucky hills.

Now, this wasn't just any mountain. It was a place thick with underbrush, overrun with copperheads and rattlers. A real snaky place—literally. Most city folks wouldn't go near it, especially not alone. But I didn't hesitate. As soon as I heard the Lord's voice, I knew it was Him. It was the same still, familiar voice I had heard as a young boy—back when I walked to the ball field alone, talking to God like He was walking right beside me. That voice hadn't changed. And when God speaks, even when His instructions are strange or uncomfortable, you know.

Besides, I knew that mountain. I knew every tree line, creek bend, and trail leading up its side. My Uncle Bill had grown up in Mullins Station, and he had taken me over just about every inch of that ground when I was younger. We'd spend hours exploring the woods, tracing the creek, climbing the ridges, and searching for the perfect spot to drop a fishing line. I looked up to him. Some of our best conversations—those "life talks"—happened right out there in the quiet of nature. He was the kind of man who didn't waste words, but what he did say always meant something.

So, as I made my way up that mountainside, memories of me and Uncle Bill came flooding back. I could still hear the crunch of leaves under our boots, the rustle of branches, and the way he'd point something out with a soft whistle. There was a peace that came with those memories—one that reminded me that I wasn't going up this mountain alone. I knew exactly which mountain God was calling me to, and I knew He was waiting for me there.

So I went with excitement, truly expecting to hear from God.

> *"Trust in the Lord with all thine heart; and lean not unto thine own understanding. In all thy ways acknowledge him, and he shall direct thy paths"*
>
> —Proverbs 3:5–6.

It was a blistering hot day. As I climbed to the top, I could feel the sun beating down on me. Once I reached the top, I found a spot overlooking the edge of the cliff, with drop-offs on my left and right, and I sat down to pray. I was seeking the Lord—truly wanting to hear from Him. As I prayed, I asked,

"Lord, would You send me a small, cool breeze just to **cool me off?**" **And He did!**

Right then and there, I felt a cool breeze sweep over me—so strong, so sudden, that I actually got cold. On that blazing mountain, where the sun had been beating down moments earlier, I now sat wrapped in a heavenly wind. It was unlike anything I'd ever experienced. Nature couldn't explain it. This was something holy—something divine.

I remained in that place for two full hours, completely surrounded by that cool, refreshing breeze. And the longer I sat there, the more I could feel it—His presence. The air itself seemed charged with holiness. I was overwhelmed that the Lord had heard such a simple prayer and responded—not with thunder or fire—but with a breeze that carried more power and tenderness than words can describe.

Some might say "chill bumps" aren't from God, but I would strongly disagree. My entire body was covered with them—wave after wave. Not from fear, but from awe. It felt like the Spirit of God was clothing me with His peace, His nearness, and His love. My heart was full. My mind was clear. For once, I wasn't distracted. I wasn't thinking about my past or my future. It was just me and God.

The best way I can describe it is this: it felt like I was already halfway to Heaven. If God had lifted me off that mountain into His glory, I would've gone with joy unspeakable. It was that real. That pure. That powerful.

There was no more weight of guilt or shame pressing on me. All the things I had repented for—the regrets, the rebellion—were no longer accusing me. I knew, deep in my spirit, that I was forgiven. Fully. It was like God was confirming it personally—not with words, but with His presence. A holy seal upon my soul.

Then, just as suddenly as it came, the breeze stopped.

The leaves that had been dancing went still. The sound of that rushing wind ceased. The stillness returned—but I was not the same.

God had met me on that mountain.

> *"Who maketh his angels spirits; his ministers a flaming fire"*
> —Psalm 104:4.

A Voice Not My Own

> *"And he said, Go forth, and stand upon the mount before the Lord. And, behold, the Lord passed by, and a great and strong wind rent the mountains... but the Lord was not in the wind... and after the wind an earthquake; but the Lord was not in the earthquake"*
> —1 Kings 19:11.

I stood up and turned to head down the mountain…

And then I heard it.

Behind me—clear and distinct—came what sounded like one long sentence in a foreign language I didn't recognize. There was no one else up there. I was completely alone.

I froze. "Lord, what in the world was that?" I said aloud. "It wasn't even in English!"

I had gone up the mountain to hear from God…

But I didn't understand what I had just heard.

(Twenty-four years later, God would call me back to this same mountain to show me even more. But in 1995, I wasn't ready for that yet.)

A fear of God came over me—not the kind of fear that drives you away, but the kind that drops you to your knees. A holy reverence. A weighty awareness that I was standing on sacred ground.

I didn't question whether God was real. I knew.

But as I stood frozen in that divine stillness, questions swirled in my mind. Was it God Himself who had spoken? Or had He sent an angel to deliver a message? I didn't know. The voice wasn't familiar. It wasn't English. It wasn't any language I understood. It came in an unknown tongue—clear, commanding, yet incomprehensible.

> *"For with stammering lips and another tongue will he speak to this people"*
> —Isaiah 28:11.

It was a mystery. And some mysteries aren't solved all at once. Some are meant to humble us, to be carried like a seed. Though I didn't receive a translation, I received something far greater: the presence of God and the conviction that Heaven had spoken. It marked me.

> *"For now we see through a glass, darkly; but then face to face…"*
> —1 Corinthians 13:12.

That evening, I shared what happened with my mom. I told her about the breeze, the stillness, and the voice.

She was deeply concerned and reminded me of dark rumors tied to that mountain. "Jeff, people say strange things happen up there—devil worship and such..."

"Mom," I said, "I know what I felt. I know what I heard. It was from God. "She didn't argue, but she didn't sleep either. She prayed.

The next morning, she walked into my room with tears in her eyes. "Jeff, the Lord gave me a word for you: **'Come.'** And He gave me Scripture." She opened her Bible and read:

> *"And the Spirit and the bride say, Come. And let him that heareth say, Come..."*
>
> —Revelation 22:17.

When she said that word—"Come"—something pierced deep into my spirit. I knew then: I hadn't heard the full sentence—I had only received the first word.

And I would carry that word for the next 26 years.

Come: The Revelation at Ellerslie

In 2021, after completing a discipleship course at Ellerslie, I stayed two extra weeks. A flat tire delayed my return to Kentucky—but God was about to reveal something that had waited over two decades.

That Tuesday, I sat at a table with young men, sharing testimonies. I said, "I once heard a word from the Lord back in 1995. The word was **'Come.'**

As I spoke it aloud, the memory came rushing back. I looked down at my open Bible—and there in the margin I read:

"Come to the Last Invitation—The Marriage Supper of the Lamb."

Tears filled my eyes. This was the full phrase I had long carried in part. I turned to Revelation 19:6–9: *"Blessed are they which are called unto the marriage supper of the Lamb..."*

Then to Revelation 22:17: *"And the Spirit and the bride say, Come..."*

It all made sense. "Come" was not just a personal call—it was a prophetic summons.

And it took a "flat tire" to keep me there until that time.

The Last Invitation – Don't Miss the Call

God's people have been given the greatest invitation ever offered—the call to the Marriage Supper of the Lamb. Jesus warned in Matthew 22 that many will ignore this call or treat it lightly. But to those who accept it, there is unspeakable joy. The question is not whether you've been invited. The question is—Will you come? We are not just guests. We are the Bride. And the Bride must make herself ready because Jesus is coming soon!

Reflection

Divine whispers don't always come with explanations. Sometimes God gives us a single word to carry for a lifetime—until the fullness of His purpose is revealed. "Come" is more than a command—it's a calling. A divine invitation to leave the familiar and step into what is eternal.

Scripture

"Blessed are they which are called unto the marriage supper of the Lamb"

—Revelation 19:9.

"And the Spirit and the bride say, Come. And let him that heareth say, Come..."

—Revelation 22:17.

Prayer

Lord, thank You for calling me to come. Even when I didn't understand, You planted that word deep in my spirit. Prepare me for what You've prepared for me. Help me to live ready—for the Marriage Supper, for Your return, and for every step of obedience between now and then. I want to be found faithful. In Jesus' name. Amen.

CHAPTER 9

Arrival and Divine Appointments

I landed in Frankfurt, Germany, on a commercial flight chartered by the Army. It was my first time in Europe, and though I had trained for this assignment, nothing fully prepares one for stepping into an entirely new world. As I exited the terminal, a wave of cold air and unfamiliarity hit me all at once—foreign signs, strange accents, and the hum of military logistics unfolding all around me. This wasn't Kentucky anymore.

My boots felt heavier than usual, and I was weighed down by a massive rucksack and two duffle bags—my entire life packed into canvas. Orders in hand, I boarded a transport to the base, heart pounding from adrenaline, uncertainty, and anticipation. It felt like I had stepped into a new chapter—a chapter I didn't fully understand yet but knew God had orchestrated.

When we arrived at the barracks, I quickly realized I was on my own. My assigned room was on the third floor, and, of course, there was no elevator. I started hauling all of my bags and gear up the steps, each step reminding me of how far I was from home. That's when I heard footsteps pounding down the hallway and a voice call out,

"Are you a newbie?" the young man asked, a wide grin on his face.

Before I could answer, he grabbed one of my duffle bags without hesitation and hoisted it over his shoulder. That was the day I met Dale Wood.

There was an instant connection—the kind that's hard to explain but even harder to ignore. It was like meeting someone you were already supposed to know. Not just a stranger offering help with a duffle bag, but a familiar soul, as if God had arranged for our paths to intersect long before either of us set foot in Germany.

Dale showed me my room and helped me with my gear. Then he said, "Come on down to my room where my friends are, and I'll introduce you." We didn't talk long—just a few exchanges about where I was from and how long I'd been in—but it didn't take much. There was no pretense, no sizing each other up like young soldiers often do. Just an open heart and an easy grin. He didn't treat me like a rookie or keep his distance like so many others. Instead, he said again, "Come on, let me introduce you to the guys."

He led me down the hallway and into his room, where several others were gathered. And just like that, I was in. There were handshakes, laughs, and warm welcomes. The room had the smell of boot polish and aftershave, with cots pushed up against the walls and gear stacked neatly in locker cabinets. It wasn't fancy—but it was family. That day, he pulled up a chair for me—not just to sit, but to belong.

He welcomed me the way you welcome a friend you've known your whole life. Not because of what I had done—but simply because he could. And I never forgot it.

Some friendships are carved not by chance, but by the hand of divine timing. They're written into your story before you even realize you're in the chapter. They're not just about camaraderie—they're about calling. Those friendships last a lifetime because they were never about the moment—they were about the mission.

"Two are better than one... for if they fall, the one will lift up his fellow"

–Ecclesiastes 4:9–10.

The Warning and the Loss

Over the next several weeks, Dale and I grew close. We worked out of the same hangar together, served on the same missions, and spent countless hours talking about life, home, and the future. He had a quiet steadiness about him. Never too loud or boastful—just solid. You could trust Dale with anything.

One warm afternoon, I was walking back from the mess hall when I saw Dale standing near the sidewalk that ran between the barracks and the hangar. His stance caught my attention—arms folded, eyes on the ground, like he was bracing for something unseen.

"Jeff... It's my turn to go on the BAB mission next week."

The Beirut Air Bridge mission wasn't routine. It involved flying high-risk diplomatic routes from Cyprus into Lebanon. Everyone respected the mission. It required more than skill—it required nerve.

But Dale wasn't rattled easily. He had a calm presence, even in chaos. Yet that day—he looked different. "I've got a bad feeling," he said. "I just... I feel like something's going to happen."

I could see it in his eyes. It wasn't anxiety. It was spiritual discernment—a holy unrest. He paused, then looked straight at me.

"Cromer, you and I... we were raised the same way. In church. We knew better. We were taught the truth. I just... I got deterred somewhere along the way."

"Dale," I said, realizing it is grace. "You've still got time. You can still choose a different path."

Then I heard Granny Hasty's voice in my heart, as clear as the day she first spoke it, and I told Dale,

"If you're ever in a place where you can't kneel and pray, just meditate on the Lord. He hears your thoughts."

"Dale," I said, "you don't need a church building to talk to Jesus. Just think on Him. Meditate on the Lord—even in silence. Even on the chopper. He hears you." He nodded, peace returning to his eyes. And then... just a few weeks later... on August 15, 1995, the call came. **Tragedy struck.**

Dale's Blackhawk helicopter went down over the Mediterranean Sea. One of the engines failed, and in the confusion, the pilot accidentally shut down the second engine. Tragically, there were no survivors.

I believe Dale remembered our conversation. Remembered his roots. Remembered Granny Hasty's words. And I believe the Lord heard him.

> *"For whosoever shall call upon the name of the Lord shall be saved"*
>
> —Romans 10:13.

> *"The Lord is nigh unto them that are of a broken heart; and saveth such as be of a contrite spirit"*
>
> —Psalm 34:18.

The funeral inside the hangar was sacred. Helmets. Rifles. Taps. Tears. No dry eyes. No hardened hearts. Dale wasn't just a soldier. He was a brother. And behind every uniform, there's a soul that will one day stand alone before the Lord.

In Memory of the Fallen

On August 15, 1995, tragedy struck over the Mediterranean Sea when a U.S. Army Blackhawk helicopter went down. Among those lost was my dear friend and brother-in-arms, SPC Dale L. Wood—a man whose friendship forever changed my life.

We also remember my other brothers, each one who carried a kind word and a steady spirit. Today, we honor the lives of all four soldiers who gave everything on that day. They were more than comrades— they were great men, and their sacrifice will never be forgotten.

CW3 Michael R. Baker, CW2 Ronald J. Cunningham SGT Robert A. Rogers, SPC Dale L. Wood

Their service, their sacrifice, and their legacy will never be forgotten. May their memory live on through the stories we tell and the lives they touched.

Cyprus: A Season of Excellence and Favor

After the tragedy, something shifted in me. I carried Dale's memory not just in sorrow, but in purpose. My time in Cyprus became a turning point.

Though I wasn't trained for it, I was asked to serve as Tech Supply Sergeant. With little prep, I dove in. I worked late, prayed for wisdom, and did it all "as unto the Lord."

"And whatsoever ye do, do it heartily, as to the Lord, and not unto men"
—Colossians 3:23.

Drawing from past jobs in Kentucky, I overhauled the inventory system. Morale improved. Losses dropped. Then came the words: "Jeff, your name is known in Washington, D.C." The favor continued. Excellence coins. Command visits. Commendation. But I knew—this wasn't about me. It was about stewardship.

"Let another man praise thee, and not thine own mouth"
— Proverbs 27:2.

*"Promotion cometh neither from the east, nor the west...
but God is the judge."*

— Psalm 75:6–7

Cyprus wasn't random. It was preparation. I didn't yet realize I was walking in the footsteps of Paul, who also proclaimed Christ here.

Angels in Cyprus

Cyprus was a place of contrasts. On the surface, it looked like paradise—whitewashed buildings, sapphire waters, the scent of olive trees drifting on the breeze. Our base was nestled near the coast, and when the skies were clear (which was often), you could look out and see the horizon stretch endlessly over the Mediterranean. But beneath that peaceful exterior, spiritual battles were quietly unfolding. And one night, I would come face-to-face with the reality that not all enemies wear uniforms.

Our commander in Cyprus was a man of God—and that, in itself, was a miracle. In the military, it's rare to encounter a commanding officer who openly lives out their faith. But this man did. He didn't just believe; he walked in it, unashamed. We had many conversations about Scripture, and he spoke about the Lord as if He were a close companion. There was something genuine and unshakable about his faith.

One day, he shared a story from his earlier years as a pilot. He had flown over the wilderness route of the Biblical Exodus, and I'll never forget what he told me. "Jeff," he said, "it's still green—even today. It's incredible to see it from the air."

That small detail left a deep impression on me. All those ancient stories we read in Scripture—they're not just allegories or symbolic lessons. They happened. In real places. On real ground. God moved across that land, and to this day, His fingerprints remain.

At the time, I had no idea that many years later, I would trace that very same Exodus route myself—visiting locations in Egypt, Jordan,

Israel, and even Saudi Arabia. But God knew. Long before I ever imagined it, He was preparing my heart for the journey.

Then came a Friday morning I'll never forget.

The commander pulled me aside privately and said, "Cromer, I haven't told the others yet, but I want to let the guys go into town tonight. They've worked hard all week, and they need a break. I want you to chaperone."

I blinked. "Sir... I'm not the highest-ranking soldier here." He smiled. "I know. But I trust you. I'll talk to the others. Whatever you say goes."

I respected him, so I agreed.

That evening, about a dozen of us climbed into "Ole Blue," our old van, and drove into town. We found a quiet little spot with outdoor seating tucked beneath a canvas awning. The air was filled with laughter as we ordered food, swapped stories, and truly relaxed for the first time in days. For a moment, all the pressure lifted. Everything felt light—peaceful, even safe. The van was parked just a few feet away, within clear view, and I remember quietly praying, *This is good for them, Lord. Thank You for this time.*

And then everything changed.

Out of nowhere, a beer bottle came flying, smashing into the side of one of my guys' heads. Blood ran down his temple as a crowd of angry locals began gathering around us. There was no warning—just chaos. Hostility filled the air like a thundercloud. The peaceful night had suddenly become dangerous.

My training kicked in. "Get in the van, now!" I ordered.

The guys moved fast—dazed, panicked, and unsure—scrambling into the van with urgency. I was the last one still outside, just about to step into the driver's seat, when something stopped me cold. It wasn't anything I saw, but I felt it. Something invisible... yet undeniable. It was as if a hand had reached out and grabbed me by the shoulders—firm, unshakable—and turned me around to face the crowd behind me.

Then I heard it.

A voice—not loud, but piercing. Quiet, yet unmistakably divine: *"Get in the van, and you die."*

It wasn't just a whisper to my ears—it was a jolt to my soul. In that moment, it felt as though the very hand of God reached down, gripped my arm, and turned me around. His presence surrounded me. It wasn't fear that stopped me—it was holy intervention. Heaven had just broken through.

God was protecting me, and I knew it.

Everything in me went still. I wasn't trembling from panic—I was arrested by the Spirit. This wasn't a thought or a gut feeling. It was a warning from the Lord Himself. And suddenly, I knew I had a choice: obey the voice... or ignore it and gamble with my life.

The others were already inside, waiting.

But I couldn't move. I couldn't take that step.

Something unseen—yet undeniably real—had just saved my life.

It wasn't fear. It wasn't confusion.

It was divine clarity. It hit so strongly, I froze mid-step, gripped by the weight of a holy presence.

God was with me.

I turned to face the crowd, took a few cautious steps toward them, and raised my hands in a gesture of peace. My voice was steady but loud enough for them all to hear.

"We're sorry if we offended any of you!" I said. "We're Americans! We're just here on vacation, trying to enjoy your beautiful island."

And it was true—what I said wasn't a lie. To all of us, Cyprus really did feel like a break, almost like a working vacation. A place to catch our breath between the pressures of deployment. Yet even though I spoke with sincerity, my words seemed to fall flat, as if they couldn't pierce the tension in the air.

The waitress raised her voice, pointing her finger sharply at the men, doing her best to drive them back. But then something shifted. I noticed it before anyone else—their eyes weren't locked on her anymore. They weren't even on me in the way I expected. Instead, their gaze was fixed past me. Not around me... but above me.

And that's when everything changed.

Their expressions shifted from hardness to confusion... then hesitation... and finally, something I'll never forget: fear.

Not fear of us. Not fear of what I had said. But fear of whatever—or whoever—they saw above me.

> *"The angel of the Lord encampeth round about them that fear him, and delivereth them"*
>
> –Psalm 34:7.

No one came closer. Not one hand was raised. No voices shouted. And just like that, the tension broke.

As I climbed back into the van, the guys looked at me and said, "Cromer, what all did you say? We had your back. We were watching."

And they meant it. My brothers weren't just talking tough—they were ready. They were following my orders to get into the van, but no doubt, my brothers were standing alert, watching every move. If that crowd had turned hostile, I know without a doubt they would've been in the fight with me.

But God took care of us that evening.

We drove away safely, without a single incident. It was as if an invisible wall had been placed between us and danger. The kind of peace you can't explain—only recognize when Heaven steps in.

> *"The angel of the Lord encampeth round about them that fear him, and delivereth them"*
>
> —Psalm 34:7.

The next morning, I called home. It wasn't always easy to connect with family overseas, but the line rang through.

My mom picked up the phone. Her voice trembled. "Honey... are you okay?"

"Yeah, Mom. Why?"

She paused, holding back tears. "God woke me up in the middle of the night. He told me you were in trouble. I couldn't see what it was—I just knew I had to pray. So, I cried out, 'Lord, send Your angels to protect my son, Jeff.'"

Goosebumps ran down my arms. I quickly checked the time difference. Her prayer—spoken from her bed back in Kentucky—was uttered at the exact hour my commander had asked me to chaperone. The very night we were surrounded.

What my mom didn't know was that her prayer became a command in Heaven. She called on protection... and God sent it.

"He shall give His angels charge over thee, to keep thee in all thy ways"
                                                    −Psalm 91:11.

"Before they call, I will answer; and while they are yet speaking, I will hear"
                                                    −Isaiah 65:24.

I believe—with everything in me—that the crowd didn't see me that night. They saw angels.

Angels who stood, weapons of light in hand, between their chaos and our safety. Angels summoned not by me, but by a mother's intercession—simple, fervent, and full of faith.

That night changed me even more. It reminded me that prayer is not passive. It is not a last resort. It is a weapon. It is a shield. It is a divine hotline to the One who commands armies of angels. And He still sends them. Not just in Bible times—but today.

Reflection

Some friendships are more than chance—they're Heaven-sent. Dale's story is a reminder that God places people in our lives with eternal purpose. Every assignment is sacred. Every trial is preparation. And every prayer—especially from a mother's heart—moves Heaven.

God is not only present in our mountaintop moments but also walks with us in hangars, supply rooms, and crowded streets. When we walk by faith, He sends provision, people, and even angels.

Scripture

> *"The angel of the Lord encampeth round about them that fear him, and delivereth them"*
>
> —Psalm 34:7.

Prayer

Lord, thank You for divine appointments—especially those we don't recognize until later. Thank You for Dale's life, his friendship, and the eternal impact he made. Help me to walk in discernment and obedience, trusting You with every step. Thank You for angels who go before us, and for mothers whose prayers never go unheard. Let my life reflect You in excellence, humility, and faith. In Jesus' name, Amen.

CHAPTER 10

Coming Home to My Foundation

Before being honorably discharged from the United States Army in January of 1998, I was offered a job at the Pentagon. I wanted to take that job! But that still small voice said, "It will change you." So, I said, "Thank you, sir, but I'm going home—to Kentucky."

Thanks to some carefully saved leave time, I was able to come home two months early. I still remember stepping off that plane—how good it felt to breathe Kentucky air again. The land looked different than where I'd been stationed, but the smell of home—fresh earth, woodsmoke, and the faint scent of pine—was something familiar, something grounding.

Granny Hasty's Bible and a Final Prayer

I was finally back near my son Jeffrey and close to my parents, siblings, and extended family. Old friends from my hometown welcomed me with open arms. I had missed so much in those years away.

But within two short weeks of returning home, Granny Hasty went home to be with the Lord. She was 81 years old. A prayer warrior. A pillar of faith. The kind of woman whose presence was felt even when she wasn't in the room.

To this day, I thank God for one of His most tender mercies: I got to see her before she passed.

Our last visit was quiet, meaningful, and full of love. We sat and talked for hours. She asked me a question that caught me off guard.

"Do you love her?" she said.

She was talking about the young, tan-legged girl I had met in Livingston—the one who had quietly captured my heart.

"Yes," I answered, without hesitation. "I do."

Then Granny looked at me with that unwavering faith in her eyes and said, "You need to marry that girl."

But I was torn. Confused. I had been raised to believe that if someone married, divorced, and remarried, they were living in sin—that remarriage meant risking your soul. And I wasn't willing to lose mine for anything.

Then Granny asked me something that stopped me in my tracks. "When you got married and divorced the first time, were you living in sin?"

"Yes," I admitted.

She nodded gently, then followed with a question that would shift everything in my heart:

"When you got saved, did God forgive you of all your sins—or all but one?"

That was a wow moment for me. Simple. Clear. And absolutely life-changing.

There was a peace in the room that day—a joy you can't manufacture. It was holy. I remember holding her fragile hand and looking into those wise, weathered eyes—eyes that had seen decades of life and loss, faith and fire. Her hands may have been frail, but her spirit was fierce. She had prayed for me through more storms than I could count.

I didn't know it would be the last time I'd see her on this side of Heaven—but God did.

After leaving her house that day, I drove across town to visit my Uncle Charles Shivel. I asked him the same question: "Do I have the right to get remarried?" And without hesitation, he gave me the same answer Granny had.

Not long after, on April 16th, 1998, we were married.

After Granny's passing, I was handed something I now treasure more than almost anything I own—her Bible.

But it wasn't just a book. It was a well-worn altar wrapped in leather. The pages were tattered, the corners curled. Countless verses were underlined; some were barely legible beneath years of notes and prayer. Scriptures were marked in fading ink. The margins were filled with handwritten petitions, and the pages—some of them—were stained with tears.

And tucked inside, folded gently between the worn pages, was a handwritten note.

It read: *"Jesus, let me see Jeff one more time before I die."*

I sat still, holding that note as its weight settled deep in my heart. God had answered her prayer. In His mercy, He gave her that one final visit—a sacred moment between a praying grandmother and her grandson. And in that visit, He used her to speak truth, to clear confusion, and to help guide the steps of my life.

That simple, handwritten plea—quietly offered in faith—had risen like incense before the Lord. And He did not ignore it. He honored it. Just two weeks before she passed, God moved through her one last time... and I will never forget it.

> *"Delight thyself also in the Lord; and he shall give thee the desires of thine heart"*
> −Psalm 37:4.

> *"The prayer of the upright is his delight"*
> −Proverbs 15:8b.

That small piece of paper, written in her familiar handwriting, became a reminder to me that God is deeply personal. He isn't just listening to the loud or eloquent prayers—He hears the whispered longings of a grandmother who simply wanted to see her grandson again.

That Bible would travel with me from season to season, and eventually, continent to continent. And though I didn't fully grasp it then, Granny's legacy was more than a family lineage—it was a spiritual inheritance.

She didn't leave behind wealth or land. She left me something far more valuable: a heart tuned to the voice of God, and a path already prayed over.

"Thy word have I hid in mine heart, that I might not sin against thee"

— Psalm 119:11.

Looking back, I realize now: I didn't just come home to my family—I came home to my foundation.

And God was only getting started.

A Dollar Store and a Costly Trap

After settling back into civilian life, I took a bold step into entrepreneurship. My first endeavor after the military was opening and operating a store called *Only a Dollar*, located in Renfro Valley, just beside my Dad's Plumbing & Electrical Store—a well-known spot in Rockcastle County that sees plenty of foot traffic and local charm. It wasn't just a job—it was a venture. An opportunity to build something of my own.

It didn't take long before the store became a local favorite. Folks came in regularly, smiling as they browsed through shelves of discounted goods. Families, seniors, out-of-town travelers—it was the kind of place that brought people together in simple ways.

I poured myself into it. I opened early. I stayed late. I made sure the store was always stocked, the floors were clean, and the customers were happy. Business was booming.

But so was my need for approval and success.

And that's when I began to fall back into a familiar pattern—workaholism.

76

I was providing for my household, yes—and the Bible says that's a good thing. But somewhere along the way, my identity got tangled in my work. I began to equate busyness with blessing, performance with purpose.

I barely had time to breathe, much less pray. My Bible reading grew thinner. My spiritual appetite dulled. Sunday mornings became less about worship and more about planning for Monday. And though everything looked stable on the outside, something was crumbling on the inside.

> *"For what is a man profited, if he shall gain the whole world, and lose his own soul?"*
>
> —Matthew 16:26.

Success isn't always a blessing if it comes at the cost of intimacy with God.

A New Opportunity: Ford Brothers Auctioneers and Realty

Not long after, I made a phone call that would shift the direction of my career—and eventually, my calling.

One day, with a stirring in my heart and a desire for something more sustainable, I picked up the phone and called Sammy Ford, co-owner with his brother Danny Ford, of Ford Brothers Auctioneers & Realtors in Mt. Vernon, who are also my cousins.

"Do you and Danny need a real estate agent?" I asked.

Without hesitation, Sammy responded, "Yes, get your real estate license and come work for us. And while you're at it, go ahead and get your auctioneer's license too."

That was all I needed to hear.

I enrolled in classes, passed my exams, and before long, I was fully licensed and officially hired by Ford Brothers in August 1999. It was a new beginning—one filled with promise.

Falling into the Same Trap Again

But once again, without realizing it, I began to overextend myself. I wasn't just trying to be good at my job—I was trying to be the best. I wanted to prove myself. I wanted to build a reputation not just as a capable real estate agent and auctioneer, but as someone you could count on for results. That drive—while admirable on the surface—began to consume me.

The late nights returned. The stress returned. And slowly but surely, so did the silence between me and God.

Church was still part of my life—some of the time—and my time with the Lord had become mechanical—routine at best, and often neglected altogether. I justified it, of course. "I'm doing good things. I'm working hard. I'm providing. God understands." And yes, He did understand—but He also wasn't satisfied with half of my heart.

> "No man can serve two masters: for either he will hate the one, and love the other... Ye cannot serve God and mammon."
> —Matthew 6:24.

> "Where your treasure is, there will your heart be also."
> —Matthew 6:21.

Success had its rewards, but it also had its cost. I was closing deals, earning commissions, gaining favor—but I was also drifting. Slowly. Quietly.

And the thing about spiritual drift is that it often doesn't feel like rebellion—it just feels like... being busy.

Reflection

It's possible to be surrounded by good things and still miss God's best. Sometimes the enemy of our calling isn't failure—it's busyness. When our hands are full of work, our hearts can quietly grow empty. God isn't looking for performance; He's after our full surrender. Even in seasons of success, He gently calls us back to the simplicity of walking with Him—hearts open, ears tuned, and lives anchored in His Word.

Scripture

"Except the Lord build the house, they labour in vain that build it: except the Lord keep the city, the watchman waketh but in vain"

–Psalm 127:1.

Prayer

Lord, thank You for the foundation of faith passed down through my family. Thank You for every reminder that success without Your presence is empty. Help me to guard my heart from distraction, and keep me anchored in Your Word. Teach me to seek You above all things, to trust Your timing, and to listen when You speak. Let my work bring You glory, and let my life reflect the legacy of those who faithfully prayed me through. In Jesus' name, Amen.

CHAPTER 11

The Whisper and the Mountain

By 2019, over twenty years had passed since my return home from the military. I was still working with Ford Brothers, still providing for my family, and by all outward measures, things were going well. I had a beautiful wife, Anissa. Three children I loved deeply. A house, a good name, and a respected position in the community. But inwardly—I was running on fumes. Work had become a treadmill I couldn't get off.

Day in and day out, I was closing deals, updating listings, running title paperwork, meeting with clients, and answering phone calls. It was like a never-ending loop. Work. Home. Church. Sleep. Repeat. I knew what the Bible said:

> *"But they that wait upon the Lord shall renew their strength..."*
> —Isaiah 40:31.

> *"Come unto Me, all ye that labour and are heavy laden, and I will give you rest"*
> —Matthew 11:28.

But I wasn't resting. I wasn't waiting on the Lord. I was grinding my way through each day, doing what I thought I was supposed to do—but forgetting to pause and ask God what He actually wanted me to do.

Then one day, a man called the office asking for advice about a legal issue tied to real estate. I wasn't sure why he reached out to me—but oddly enough, I had just dealt with a similar situation and was able to guide him step by step. We hung up the phone, and I felt good that I'd helped someone.

But then, I got up, walked over to the front door of the office, and looked outside.

That's when the Holy Spirit spoke to my heart. Not audibly—but so clearly, it arrested me in my tracks:

"If you knew My Word as well as you know man's law... then you would be a good man."

The weight of those words hit me like a freight train.

I knew real estate law, property values, contract language—I could walk a client through a closing with my eyes closed. But God wasn't impressed by my knowledge of contracts or commissions.

He wanted my heart.
He wanted my hunger back.
He wanted me.

"Study to shew thyself approved unto God, a workman that needeth not to be ashamed..."
—2 Timothy 2:15.

"The entrance of thy words giveth light; it giveth understanding unto the simple"
—Psalm 119:130.

For a moment, I just stood there—staring out the door, thinking of all my hard work and what I had built, realizing that somewhere along the way... I had stopped building on the Rock.

"Except the Lord build the house, they labour in vain that build it..."

—Psalm 127:1.

I whispered a simple prayer under my breath:

"Lord... there's got to be more."

That prayer wasn't long—but it was real. It came from a man who was tired of walking in circles. A man who was ready to step off the treadmill and onto whatever path God had next.

The Call to the Mountain

The very next day, as I sat behind the same desk, with the same schedule, and the same stack of to-dos...

I heard the Lord speak again.

This time, He said, **"Pack a backpack. Buy a plane ticket. And come see the place where the Lord lay."**

The next morning, I returned to work, fully expecting a packed schedule. There were contracts to finalize, phone calls to return, and real estate paperwork that needed immediate attention. But even as I settled into the familiar rhythm of my day, I felt a divine interruption.

Clear as a bell, the Lord spoke to my heart:

"Go to the mountain."

It wasn't a whisper. It wasn't subtle. It was direct. Firm. Immediate. The kind of instruction that feels like it cuts through the noise of life.

I knew exactly what mountain He meant. Mullins Station. The same place He had sent me back in 1995 before I deployed to Germany. That mountain had once been thick with underbrush, home to copperheads and rattlers, and yet it was sacred ground—holy because God had met me there before.

But this time, **I hesitated.**

"Lord, I can't just drop everything," I reasoned. "I've got a full slate today. I've got work to do." That's when I felt another strong impression—so precise, it stopped me mid-thought:

"10:00 a.m."

Now that got my attention. He wasn't just telling me what to do. He was telling me when to do it. Still, I pushed back in my mind. "That's just forty-five minutes from now. There's no way I can wrap everything up and make it out there that fast. I've got too much going on."

Then the Spirit gently nudged me again with a third instruction:

"Take the documents to the attorneys now."

So I did. I grabbed the closing files and headed to the law office, mentally preparing for what usually turns into long conversations about deals, listings, and auctions. But when I arrived, both attorneys were out. No one stopped me to chat. No one delayed me. I was in and out in five minutes.

"In all thy ways acknowledge him, and he shall direct thy paths"
—Proverbs 3:6.

And that's exactly what He was doing—clearing a divine path.

Still unsure, I returned to the office and tried to go back to my list. "Lord, I've still got that house to list today," I argued.

Another nudge came, soft but undeniable:

"Call the lady."

So I picked up the phone and dialed. "Jeff! I was just getting ready to call you!" she answered. "My husband and I decided to leave for Florida today. We'll call you when we get back."

It was like watching dominoes fall in perfect order. The Lord had cleared every single task from my morning. Every excuse I had just evaporated. That's when I knew: God was serious.

And I needed to move.

The Encounter on the Mountain

I arrived at the base of the mountain at exactly 9:40 a.m.

The air was still, almost too quiet—like the earth itself was holding its breath. The gravel crunched beneath my shoes as I stepped out of the car, and for a moment, I just stood there, staring at the muddy trail in front of me.

The ground was wet from the previous night's rain. The ditch between the road and the base of the mountain was slick and muddy. I had on dress clothes—new shoes, clean pants, a tucked-in shirt, and tie. I looked more like I was headed to a real estate appointment than a hike into holy ground.

"Lord, I'm not dressed for this," I muttered. "My shoes will be ruined if I jump this ditch. My pants will get filthy if I kneel to pray."

That's when the Lord spoke again—not a still, small voice. It was thunder in my spirit. Clear. Strong. Unmistakable:

> *"You asked for more. I'm going to show you more. I'm asking you to go to the top of the mountain and pray. It's your decision. Right here. Right now. What's it going to be?*

I WILL NOT PASS THIS WAY AGAIN."

His words hit me like a tidal wave. My heart began to race. I had begged God to show me more. I had cried out, worn down from work and worry, asking for a deeper encounter. And here He was—calling me higher. Calling me to lay down my comfort, my pride, my excuses—and climb.

> *"I have set before you life and death, blessing and cursing: therefore choose life..."*
>
> —Deuteronomy 30:19.

So, I made my choice.

I ran across the road and jumped the ditch. My shoes sank into the mud. That small voice said, **"Don't look down."**

So, I kept my eyes up and my heart open. I pressed forward, brushing past thorny branches and climbing the rugged trail, step by step. With every stride, something in me broke free—fear, resistance, the urge to stay in control. I wasn't just climbing a mountain. I was surrendering on one.

Heavenly Vision: Golgotha and the Face of Jesus

When I reached the summit, I fell to my knees. Then to my face.

The ground was damp and earthy. The scent of leaves and wet dirt filled my lungs. My knees pressed into the soil. But none of that mattered anymore. I was in the presence of God.

> *"Who shall ascend into the hill of the Lord? or who shall stand in His holy place? He that hath clean hands, and a pure heart..."*
>
> —Psalm 24:3–4.

I wept. I repented. I worshipped.

I cried out, "Lord, what did You mean when You said 'Come' back in 1995? What are You trying to show me now?"

Then I said something I'll never forget: "Lord, I'm probably the only man in Rockcastle County standing on top of a mountain right now, talking to You. You called me. Will You show me something?"

I waited. Silence.

Then I prayed, "Lord, just send a breeze if You're near."

And He did.

The wind picked up just slightly, a soft breeze wrapping around me like a Heavenly whisper. It cooled my skin and warmed my heart, just like He did back in 1995.

I continued in prayer, but there was only silence. Nothing. Not even one word. Then, as I was standing up, I said, "Lord, I know you called me here to tell me something or to show me something. What is it?"

Still, nothing.

I turned to leave the mountaintop, feeling a strange mix of reverence and restlessness. I had knelt. I had prayed. I had obeyed. And God had met me there with that cool breeze.

But I wasn't ready to go—not yet.

I lifted my hands one more time and declared aloud,

"Lord, I'm not much of a man... but I'm here, Lord!"

The clouds above me were thick and gray, with no sign of sunlight anywhere. The sky was covered—solid and dull. But as I stood there beneath those trees, something began to shift.

Right above me, between the trees, the clouds opened.

What appeared wasn't just a break in the clouds—it was a perfect circle of brilliant blue sky. Not a misshapen break or an irregular gap. It was flawless in shape. So perfect it looked drawn by the hand of God Himself.

I froze.

Then, right inside that circular window in the sky, the clouds began to move and swirl, shaping themselves into a familiar image—something unmistakable.

A skull.

The sight startled me. The hollow eyes, the defined cheekbones, the ominous stillness of it all. I hunkered down instinctively, gripped by both awe and fear. I had my phone in my hand, but I couldn't bring myself to lift it. It was as if God had told me, "This isn't for pictures—it's for your soul."

The skull began to fade like mist... and then another image took shape inside the same blue window.

This time, it was a face.

But not just any face.

It was His.

Gentle. Detailed. The face of Jesus.

My breath caught in my chest. I couldn't move. I couldn't speak. All I could do was... behold.

The contrast between the two images—the skull and the Savior—was overwhelming. One represented death. The other, life. One was the symbol of suffering, the other of resurrection power.

Suddenly, the Spirit whispered to my heart:

"That was Golgotha. The place of the skull." It all made sense.

"And when they were come unto a place called Golgotha, that is to say, a place of a skull..."
—Matthew 27:33.

Then I heard another whisper deep in my spirit:

"I will send a man."

I responded, audibly, "A man, Lord? There are many men. How will I know?"

And the reply came again, steady and clear:

"A man... with a beard."

I didn't know what that meant—yet. But I knew I had heard Him. And I knew that the encounter wasn't over.

Clean Shoes and a Confirming Vision

As I made my way down the trail and to my car, my thoughts spinning, I glanced down at my clothes, expecting to see the evidence of mud and dampness from the climb.

But to my utter amazement, my shoes were spotless.

My pants were clean.

There wasn't a trace of mud on me.

I had knelt in wet ground, trudged through mud and brush—and yet, I looked untouched.

In that moment, I was reminded of Jude 1:24:

"Now unto Him that is able to keep you from falling, and to present you faultless..."

The Holy Spirit whispered once again:

"You've been washed. You've been covered. Just like your shoes... I've kept you clean."

Tears welled up in my eyes.

God had shown me something holy that day—not just in the sky, but in my heart. And though I hadn't yet grasped the full meaning, I knew this: He was calling me to something greater.

Something eternal.

I drove back to the office in silence.

There was no music playing. No phone calls. Just the sound of my tires humming over the road as my heart replayed everything I had seen on the mountain—

The skull.

The face of Jesus.

The perfect circle of blue sky.

And the whispered words:

"I will send a man... with a beard."

A Vision Confirmed

I was still trembling with wonder. Not from fear, but from reverence. I didn't yet understand the full meaning of what had happened, but I knew I had encountered the Holy.

When I arrived back at Ford Brothers, I walked into the office almost cautiously. Everything felt different. My surroundings hadn't changed—but I had. My eyes had seen something eternal, and I carried a weight of glory in my soul that could not be shaken off.

I sat down at my desk and stared out the window.

That's when it happened.

I saw it—clear as day. **A tomb**. Right outside.

Not in the distance. Not in a dream. But right outside my office window, in the Spirit. I wasn't asleep. I wasn't imagining things. It was a vision—just as real to me as the desk I was sitting at.

It stopped me in my tracks.

This wasn't just a random image. I had never seen this tomb before, yet somehow, I recognized it.

Quietly, I whispered, *"Lord... what is this?"*

On that particular day, a pastor's wife was filling in as the secretary. Knowing she would understand, I told her about the vision I had just seen. Without hesitation, she said, "Jeff, I have a good friend who is in Israel right now, and she just sent me this picture."

I walked over slowly, still caught up in the awe of what I had just experienced. She held up her phone. And I froze.

It was the same tomb.

The exact same tomb I had seen in the vision only moments before. Every detail matched—the stone doorway, the garden setting, even the angle from which I had seen it in my spirit. It wasn't just similar—it was a divine confirmation.

I asked her, "Where is that?"

She smiled. "It's the Garden Tomb, just outside Jerusalem."

The very place believed by many to be where Jesus was crucified, buried... and where He rose again.

> *"He is not here, for He is risen, as He said. Come, see the place where the Lord lay"*
>
> —Matthew 28:6.

The Call to Israel

God was calling me to go to Israel. Not on a tour. Not for a vacation. Not as a bucket-list trip.

But as a divine assignment. A pilgrimage. A walk of obedience into the very places where Jesus walked. And He had confirmed it with a vision, a mountain encounter, a clear word, and now—a literal picture.

God had ordered every step.

"This is the Lord's doing; it is marvellous in our eyes"
—Psalm 118:23.

Everything I had experienced in the past few days had led to this undeniable conclusion: God was calling me. Not in theory—but in reality.

The vision of the tomb.

The exact image sent from Israel that same day.

The face in the clouds.

The clearings in my schedule.

The echo of the word **"Come."**

There was no more room for doubt.

The same Lord who spoke to Moses from a burning bush…

The same Lord who led Elijah to Mount Horeb…

The same Lord who called Paul to Macedonia in a dream…

…was now calling me to the Holy Land.

And I had a decision to make.

Not just about travel plans or airline tickets—but about obedience.

Would I trust Him completely?

"Trust in the Lord with all thine heart; and lean not unto thine own understanding. In all thy ways acknowledge him, and he shall direct thy paths."
—Proverbs 3:5–6

As I sat quietly, a deep sense of peace came over me—not the kind the world offers, but the peace that only comes from knowing you've heard from Heaven.

My heart whispered, "Yes, Lord. I'll go."

Not because it made sense. Not because I had it all figured out. Not because I had the money or itinerary. But because I had heard His voice.

"My sheep hear my voice, and I know them, and they follow me"

—John 10:27.

That evening, I told Anissa everything. She listened quietly, her eyes filling with tears—not of fear, but of confirmation. She had been sensing something, too. The Lord had been preparing her heart as well.

"I believe you're supposed to go," she said.

And with that, the path was set.

Because what God was about to do in my life would forever change me.

That journey would soon become the heartbeat of this book.

But it started here. On a Kentucky mountain. With a whispered call, a perfect blue circle in the clouds, and the face of Jesus staring back at me.

Reflection

God doesn't just call the qualified—He qualifies the called. When we slow down long enough to hear His voice, we find that He's been speaking all along. In our busy lives, His still small whisper can become the invitation to a life we never imagined. And when we say yes to Him, the impossible becomes a divine assignment.

Scripture

"And thine ears shall hear a word behind thee, saying, This is the way, walk ye in it..."
—Isaiah 30:21.

Prayer

Father, thank You for speaking, even when I've been too distracted to listen. Forgive me for the times I've ignored Your whispers or chosen comfort over obedience. Open my ears to hear You clearly and my heart to follow without delay. Give me the courage to step into the unknown, knowing that wherever You lead, You provide. In Jesus' name, Amen.

CHAPTER 12

A Faith That Walks

Some lessons from God don't come in a classroom or a church pew—they come on the road, when you're willing to walk by faith and not by sight. After the mountaintop encounter in 2019, I knew the Lord was calling me deeper. But I didn't realize how much He was about to strip away—my plans, my comforts, even my phone—until all that remained was trust. Not just belief. Not just church talk. But the kind of faith that packs a bag, boards a plane, and steps into the unknown because God said, **"Come."**

It was no longer enough to say I believed. He was calling me to walk what I believed.

> *"For we walk by faith, not by sight"*
> —2 Corinthians 5:7.

That week after the mountain was filled with an unusual sense of anticipation. I couldn't explain it, but something was stirring in my spirit. Every morning felt like an invitation to lean in a little closer. I found myself waking up early, praying longer, listening more intently. The Lord didn't give me the full picture—He gave me something better: the awareness that He was preparing me for something sacred. I didn't know the steps, but I knew the Shepherd. And when you follow the Good Shepherd, you don't need to see the map—you only need to trust the voice.

> *"My sheep hear my voice, and I know them, and they follow me"*
>
> —John 10:27.

The Woman Who Prayed

That following weekend, I joined a small group heading to a church service in neighboring Jackson County. It wasn't a formal plan—just one of those Spirit-led days where you knew you were supposed to go. But before we made it to the church, the pastor in the group suggested we stop by the home of an elderly woman who was too sick to attend.

I had never met her before, but the moment we stepped inside her modest home, I felt the peace of God. The living room was simple, yet filled with the presence of someone who had spent a lifetime with the Lord. You could almost feel her prayers hanging in the air like a gentle fragrance.

As we prepared to leave, the pastor turned to her and said, "Would you pray for Jeff? He's preparing to go to Israel."

She didn't hesitate.

This dear woman of God reached out her frail hand, placed it gently on my shoulder, and began to pray. Then something happened.

Her voice began to tremble as the Spirit of God took over. She began to speak in tongues, and then, with clarity and authority, she gave the interpretation:

> *"I will keep you safe during your travels. There shall not a hair of your head be harmed. I require your time."*

That last phrase gripped me—*I require your time.*

It pierced straight through my heart. I knelt there, stunned and unable to speak. Why would the Almighty God—the Creator of Heaven and Earth—desire my time? I wasn't a preacher. I didn't see myself as especially gifted or qualified. I was just a man trying to be obedient, yet slipping back again and again into what *self* wanted, or thought I could do.

But in that moment, I understood: God wasn't merely asking for my time—He was reminding me that it already belonged to Him. Scripture says, *"Ye are not your own, for ye are bought with a price"* (1 Corinthians 6:19–20). My time, my strength, my very life had been purchased by the blood of Christ.

And then the words of Jesus echoed in my spirit: *"Without me ye can do nothing"* (John 15:5). How often had I drifted back into the ways of self, leaning on my own strength, chasing what the flesh could accomplish? The flesh profits nothing—it cannot produce what only the Spirit of God can bring forth.

I realized that every time I returned to self-reliance, I was stepping away from the very source of life. Jesus had already told us plainly: apart from Him, there is no fruit, no power, no lasting work. Only through abiding in Him could my life bear the kind of fruit that remains.

That night, the Spirit of God was not just correcting me—He was inviting me. Inviting me to surrender my time, my will, and my strength, not as a burden, but as an offering. For when God requires something, it is not to take from us, but to give us more of Himself in return.

So, I asked, quietly in my heart, "Lord, why don't You just tell me the whole story now? Why do I have to go all the way to Israel to learn what You want me to know? You're the same God here as You are there!"

And the Holy Spirit whispered:

So that I can teach you. If I told you more than one word, you'd forget it and learn nothing.

It was humbling. But it made perfect sense. God teaches us step by step, not all at once—because trust grows in the walking, not by talking and talking, but doing!

The Man with the Beard

Just a few days after that powerful prayer from the elderly woman, I attended a Spirit-filled men's retreat. I didn't go expecting a word from the Lord—just some good worship, fellowship, and time away from my normal routine. But God had something more in mind.

The atmosphere that evening was thick with the presence of God. Worship had settled the room into a holy stillness, the kind that invites Heaven to speak. I sat quietly at one of the tables, my Bible open in front of me, listening.

That's when I saw him—a man I didn't know, standing on the other side of the room. He looked like he was wrestling with something. Then, slowly, he began walking toward me. He was tall, had a thick beard, and an expression that said he was unsure if he should even be coming.

As he walked toward me and bent over to speak, he hesitated. "I started not to come over here," he said quietly, "but the Lord told me I had to. He said to tell you…"

He paused,

"*Out of your belly shall flow rivers of living water.*"

The moment he spoke those words, I felt the power of God rush over me. It wasn't just prophecy—it was confirmation. This was the man God had promised me back on the mountain when I cried out, "Lord, show me something!" and the clouds had parted in the shape of a skull, then the face of Jesus. That day, God had said, "*I will send a man. A man with a beard.*"

Here he was—standing right in front of me.

"He that believeth on me, as the scripture hath said, out of his belly shall flow rivers of living water"

—John 7:38.

I couldn't speak. I just nodded and thanked him. I didn't need an explanation. I knew it was from the Lord.

Later that night, I went outside alone and looked up at the sky. "Lord," I whispered, "You're really doing this, aren't You?"

That verse about the rivers stayed with me. I didn't fully understand it, but I knew that it was about more than emotion. It was about overflow—a life so filled with Christ that His Spirit pours out through your very being.

"And the Lord shall guide thee continually, and satisfy thy soul in drought... thou shalt be like a watered garden... whose waters fail not"

—Isaiah 58:11.

Called to Radical Trust

In the days following that men's retreat, I couldn't shake the feeling that God was preparing me for something far beyond a casual trip. This wasn't about a vacation to the Holy Land—it was a spiritual assignment. The kind of mission that would demand everything I had.

Each time I prayed, I heard the same thing over and over in my spirit: ***"Trust Me."***

At first, I thought it meant trust Him to get me there and back safely. But the longer I listened, the clearer the message became:

Trust Me for everything: food, water, shelter, direction, and people.

The Lord was not just asking me to believe—He was asking me to walk out that belief.

97

"For we walk by faith, not by sight"
—2 Corinthians 5:7.

No Itinerary, No Phone

I felt the Lord saying:

- No itinerary.
- No reservations.
- No backup plan.
- No distractions.
- No cell phone.

That last one caught me off guard. No phone, Lord? How will I navigate? How will I call home? What if I get lost? So many questions, but God was wanting my Trust in Him.

He gently reminded me of the mountain. On that hill in Mullins Station, it was just me and Him—no calls, no GPS, no outside voices, just Trust. And that's how He wanted it to be again.

"As the Father hath sent me, even so send I you"
—John 20:21.

God wasn't calling me to tour Israel—He was calling me to walk with Him there. He wanted full surrender. And full surrender required trust.

Packing Light

At first, I bought new luggage—nice rolling suitcases. I figured if I was going overseas, I should at least be prepared. But as I stood there in my room, admiring the bags, I heard the Lord again:

No luggage. Just a backpack. Keep your hands free.

Hands free for what? I didn't know. Maybe to help someone. Maybe to receive something. Maybe to hold onto nothing but Him.

> *Provide neither gold, nor silver... nor scrip for your journey... for the workman is worthy of his meat.*
> —Matthew 10:9–10

The instructions came one by one:

- Eat what is put in front of you.
- Sleep where I lead.
- Don't ask others what to do.
- Trust no man.
- Don't put your confidence in man.
- Listen to no man.
- **Listen to Me alone.**

It felt like a divine scavenger hunt—but the prize wasn't a destination, it was intimacy with Jesus.

A Trip to the Courthouse

So, I obeyed. I bought a sturdy backpack. Packed three changes of clothes. My Bible. No plans. No hotels. No reservations. And no phone.

That's when God gave me another nudge. One that seemed odd at the time:

"Go to the Courthouse and get a copy of your DD-214."

My military discharge form? Why would I need that in Israel?

But I didn't question—I obeyed. I walked across the street to the Rockcastle County Courthouse, unsure what I'd even tell them. The women at the clerk's office were kind and helpful. One of them asked, "Why do you need this form?"

"I'm going to Israel," I said.

99

Her eyes widened. "By yourself?"

"Yes. Just me."

She asked, "Aren't you scared?"

I didn't even hesitate. It was like the words leaped out of my mouth before I had time to think.

"No, I believe that if any man lays a hand on me, the Lord will take his breath away!"

Everyone in the room paused.

And even I was surprised by the confidence in my voice.

Walking back to my office, I smiled and added a little prayer just between me and the Lord:

"Lord, You don't have to hurt anybody because of me. I don't want You to take any man's breath away... but if You could just take his breath for about fifteen seconds so I can get away, that'd be fine."

I knew He understood my humor—and more importantly, He understood my heart.

Voices of Doubt

As word spread that I was preparing to leave for Israel—with no itinerary, no hotel, no phone, and only a backpack—it didn't take long for the questions to start. And it wasn't just strangers. It was people who loved me—church folks, family, coworkers. People who genuinely wanted the best for me and were concerned about my safety.

I understood their concern, but I couldn't let "safety" stand in the way of the opportunities God was preparing to place before me.

"Where there is no vision, the people perish..."
—Proverbs 29:18.

One evening after a midweek service, I stood outside the church with a small group. The sun was setting behind the steeple. Someone asked casually, "So, Jeff, when are you flying out?"

"In a few weeks," I said.

"Do you have your hotel booked yet?"

"No," I said plainly. "The Lord told me not to make reservations."

There was a moment of silence. Then came the awkward laughs.

"Wait... what?"

"I'm going by faith."

Some tried to laugh it off. Others looked genuinely concerned. One brother even pulled me aside and said, "Jeff, I think you're letting your emotions get ahead of your wisdom. You're a husband, a father... This isn't just about you."

I nodded. I appreciated his concern. But I also knew this wasn't just about me—it was about **obedience.**

> *"The fear of man bringeth a snare: but whoso putteth his trust in the Lord shall be safe"*
>
> —Proverbs 29:25.

I said to this man, *"I believe the Lord will have someone waiting on me at the airport."*

I could hear the murmurs. I could feel the doubt in the room. Some thought I was crazy.

The next day at work, Sam called me into his office. He looked at me across the desk like a father talking to a son who's about to make a big mistake.

"Jeff, you really need to plan this out," he said gently. "You can't just fly to the Middle East without a guide. What are you going to do, just go there and sit?"

I smiled and said, "I know. But the Lord told me to trust Him."

"You don't want to get there and be wandering around. It's dangerous. It's unpredictable," Sam said.

He meant well. I knew that. And honestly, part of me wanted to take his advice. My flesh wanted comfort. My mind wanted logic. But my spirit knew better.

> *"For my thoughts are not your thoughts, neither are your ways my ways, saith the Lord"*
> —Isaiah 55:8.

That's when Danny stepped in.

"I've got a couple that I'm working with who has been to Israel multiple times," he said. "They know a local guide in Jerusalem. Maybe God is trying to help you through them."

He was sincere. Thoughtful. Trying to help.

Then he added, "There's a fine line between having faith and being stupid."

The next day, Danny handed me a slip of paper with their contact info.

I hesitated—but eventually called the pastor's wife. She was kind and encouraging, and she gave me the tour guide's email. So, I wrote:

"I'll be in Israel for 15 days. What do you charge for your services?"

Then I prayed:

"Lord, if this is not from You, let the response be so high that I'll know without a doubt You're still leading me to go alone."

A day later, the email came back:

- Airport pickup?
- Lodging: $200 per day
- Tour guide: $400 per day
- Rental car: $300 per day
- Meals not included

That was over $15,000 for 15 days—not including flights.

I walked into Danny's office and explained what the tour guide had said and how much it would cost.

Danny looked at me in disbelief. *"Are you serious? He wanted to charge you that much—for fifteen days?"* He shook his head.

I smiled. *"I told you, I'm going to Israel by faith."*

Final Preparations & Confirmations

As the departure date drew closer, my heart was steady—but my mind was still catching up.

I would sit at my desk at the office, going through contracts or title paperwork, and quietly pray, "Lord, I'm still listening. Am I doing this right?" And each time, He would answer. Not with thunder, not with lightning. But with peace.

> *"And let the peace of God rule in your hearts, to the which also ye are called in one body; and be ye thankful"*
> —Colossians 3:15.

That peace became my compass. I didn't feel frantic. I didn't feel the need to prepare more than I had. I just kept walking, one obedient step at a time. Pack the bag. Print your documents. Wait on Me. He even prompted me again to take the DD-214. In hindsight, it was part of His perfect foresight. I didn't need all the answers. I just needed to obey.

Traveling Light

Packing was simple. I had a backpack, a Bible, three sets of clothes, a camera, some cash, and a credit card. I left behind everything unnecessary—including fear.

I remember looking at the empty space in my pack and thinking, *This feels so backwards... so unprepared.*

But God reminded me that this was a different kind of journey.

"Provide neither gold, nor silver, nor brass in your purses, nor scrip for your journey... for the workman is worthy of his meat"

—Matthew 10:9–10.

This trip wasn't about tourism. It was about trust. It wasn't about what I could carry—but about what I was willing to let go of.

A Conversation with My Wife

Before I left, I sat down with my wife, Anissa. I knew the Lord had given her peace early on, but I still wanted to make sure. "Honey, are you still okay with this? With me not having a phone? No set schedule?" She looked at me without hesitation and said, "God gave me peace when you told me the Lord called you. I've had no fear since. I know He'll keep you." And that was one of the most powerful confirmations I could've received.

We prayed together. We wept. And we trusted.

The Day Before Departure

The night before my flight, I couldn't sleep. Not from worry—but from a holy anticipation. I got out of bed and walked outside into the crisp Kentucky night air. The stars were so clear—no clouds, just a quiet, moonlit sky.

"Lord," I whispered, "I don't know what's waiting on the other side of this trip. But I believe You are." I lifted my hands and surrendered it all again. The planning. The safety. The timing. The outcome. All of it. Then I heard in my spirit:

"For we walk by faith, not by sight"

—2 Corinthians 5:7.

I closed my eyes and whispered: "I'm ready."

Reflection

Faith isn't proven on the mountaintop—it's proven in motion. This chapter was more than a journey of travel; it was a journey of total surrender. To trust God when you can't see the next step is to walk the way Jesus did—by faith. God isn't looking for well-prepared tourists. He's looking for surrendered disciples.

Scripture

"Trust in the Lord with all thine heart; and lean not unto thine own understanding. In all thy ways acknowledge Him, and He shall direct thy paths"
—Proverbs 3:5–6.

Prayer

Father, thank You for calling us beyond comfort into deep trust. Teach us to hear Your voice and to follow even when we cannot see. Strip away our fear, our need for control, and every plan not authored by You. May our hands stay free, and our hearts stay fixed on You. Give us courage to walk by faith and not by sight. In Jesus' name, Amen.

CHAPTER 13

By Faith and Not by Sight

People have often commented on how courageous I was to travel to Israel on absolute faith—with no itinerary, no cell phone, just my Bible, the clothes on my back, three changes of clothes in my backpack, a camera, my DD-214, some cash, and a credit card.

But it was actually my wife, Anissa, who was the brave one. We had many conversations about my upcoming trip. Secretly, I asked the Lord to give her a deep and abiding peace. As my departure got closer, I asked her directly:

"Honey, do you have peace? Are you still okay with this—with not being able to contact me or know where I am until you pick me up at the airport?"

"Yes," she assured me. "God has given me His peace. I know this is what He wants you to do."

So I had all green lights to go!

Air Travel Day – July 7, 2019

A friend of mine drove me to the Lexington airport in my brand-new truck. His wife was pregnant at the time. I told him to keep my truck and drive it while I was gone because he would need it to take his wife to the hospital. And that's exactly what happened. He hadn't planned on using my truck—but that's what they ended up needing.

My flight schedule would take me from Lexington to Chicago to Munich, and finally to Tel Aviv.

God had impressed on me to carry my Bible outside my backpack in every airport and on every flight.

I finally understood why He told me to pack light and keep my hands free.

Though we took off in the early morning hours, I was too keyed up to rest. I read my Bible and reflected on all the ways God had led me to this moment. I felt deeply humbled and grateful.

The Enemy's Whisper

During the flight from Chicago to Munich, the enemy crept in.

You fool. God isn't going to have anybody waiting on you. Do you really think you'll make it back home? You are SO stupid.

I trembled. I listened—at first. Then I opened my Bible.

> *"Thou shalt not tempt the Lord thy God"*
> —Deuteronomy 6:16a.

I didn't want to tempt God by not trusting Him. After about five minutes, the devil left me alone.

In that moment, I realized something powerful: being on that plane felt like being in Christ. I was surrounded by the strong materials of the plane, yes—but more than that, I was surrounded by the covering of God. Nothing—absolutely nothing—could touch me unless God allowed it.

> *"My sheep hear my voice, and I know them, and they follow me: And I give unto them eternal life; and they shall never perish, neither shall any man pluck them out of my*

hand. My Father, which gave them me, is greater than all; and no man is able to pluck them out of my Father's hand. I and my Father are one"

—John 10:27–30.

A Divine Exchange in Germany

At the airport in Munich, I had to go through customs in a small room. Armed guards patrolled above on a mezzanine. A female agent questioned me harshly, clearly irritated by my Bible.

"Why do you want to go to Israel?"

"Why only a backpack?"

"What kind of book is that?"

"You don't even know where you're staying?"

She mocked my answers and made fun of my Bible.

I answered each question honestly and politely, but finally, I'd had enough. I turned my head slightly and whispered:

"Lord, I am done dealing with this woman. I don't want to talk to her anymore."

Immediately, a man in a suit walked behind the counter and replaced her. He asked a few questions. I asked one of my own:

"Are you part of the German Army?"

"Yes, I am."

"Sir, I don't understand. Why all the questions? It's a Bible. I served here in Giebelstadt from 1995 to 1998. I have a copy of my DD-214. Would you like to see it?"

"Yes, I would."

I handed it to him. He looked at it and said:

"We're brothers."

He scribbled something on a piece of paper, clipped it to my passport, and said:

"Have a good day."

Once again, God showed up and showed off. That DD-214 the Lord told me to carry? It opened the door.

I boarded the bus that took me to my plane. As I walked up the steps to board the plane, I glanced over and saw that same suited man standing nearby, watching to make sure I got on.

The Bold Declaration

When my flight from Germany to Israel took off, I knew: this was the point of no return.

This was also the noisiest leg of the journey. Everyone seemed to be talking—except me. I kept my Bible open.

Then a young man leaned across the aisle and said:

"Excuse me, sir. Tell me your favorite verse—right here, right now!"

My mind went completely blank. But then, loudly—over the noisy cabin—I declared:

"WE WALK BY FAITH, NOT BY SIGHT"
—2 Corinthians 5:7.

In the instant before I spoke, the plane went totally silent. You could hear a pin drop. Everyone nearby heard my declaration.

The young man shivered and said, **"Ooh, that is good!"**

Arrival in Israel

We flew over Cyprus, and memories of my military time came rushing back. I also thought about my first few hours in Israel during that Mediterranean cruise years ago. This time, I'd have 15 whole days.

I had asked the Lord, "How long should I stay in Jerusalem?" Then I opened to Galatians 1:18:

"Then after three years I went up to Jerusalem to see Peter, and abode with him fifteen days."

So, the total trip would be 17 days:

- 2 for travel
- 15 days in Jerusalem

Where's the Help?

On the plane, I met a man traveling with his little boy. We talked and learned we were both going to Jerusalem. He had a car waiting.

I thought: Here is the man that I believed God would have at the airport to help me.

As we walked toward the exit of the airport, I waited for him to invite me to ride with him. But it never happened.

"Have a safe trip," he said. "You too," I replied. He went left. I walked straight out the front door. My heart sank. What am I going to do? But even then—no fear. Just certainty. I was supposed to take a bus.

Then God said to my spirit, "You can secure My Word now."

I slipped my Bible into the front pouch of my backpack, and that still small voice said:

"Out of all the thousands of people you've seen pass by, how many had their hands free to hold a Bible? How many were reading My Word?"

None, Lord.

And you asked, "Why me?"

I thought, *Oh, wow! What a profound statement!*

(At the time, I didn't completely understand what God had planned for me, but during the writing of this book, the Lord gave me another thought... **A Bible in Every Hand!**)

I said, "Lord, I sure believed that You would have someone here at the airport waiting on me..."

That sweet, still, small voice said, "You said 'AT' the airport, not 'IN' the airport!"

My jaw dropped once again.

The Bicycle Man

I approached a sign outside the airport. To the left: taxis.

I asked a man, "Where can I catch the bus to Jerusalem?"

"Not this sign… not the next… the third."

The number three.

Father, Son, Holy Ghost.

It was a beautiful day—clear skies, a light breeze, not too hot. At the third sign, I noticed a man standing with a bicycle. I walked up to him.

"Hey, how are you doing?"

"Fine. How are you?" He spoke English.

"Where are you from?"

"Kentucky."

"What do you do in Kentucky?"

"I sell real estate."

"Well, I buy real estate."

He explained that he owned rental units and leased them to the U.S. Embassy in Jerusalem. Normally, he said, he took the train with his bike.

"But today—for security reasons—they made me get off at the airport and take the bus."

"That's never happened before," he added.

Right then, I knew: this was the man I had believed God would send to me.

"I think I know the reason you're here," I told him quietly. "I believe God sent you to me."

He smiled. "Perhaps."

He asked if I had a place to stay. I told him no. "If I had a rental available, you could stay there," he said.

The bus door opened. I tried to pay, but the driver kept saying, "Shekel! Shekel!"

I turned to the man with the bike. "He keeps saying 'shekel.'"

"He's asking for money."

"I've got money."

"But you need shekels."

He exchanged a hundred dollars for me and handed me 360 shekels—a fair rate. I paid the driver 18 shekels for the ride and boarded.

Guided to Jaffa Street

Bike Man sat down beside me, and we continued talking.

"If you Google 'places to stay in Jerusalem,' a bunch will pop up," he said.

"I don't have a cell phone."

His eyes widened. "What? You don't have a cell phone?"

"No. I'm traveling with no distractions."

He pulled out his phone and found a $150-per-night hotel. "I've heard about hostels," I said.

"You'd stay at a hostel?"

"Yes."

"There's one at 44 Jaffa Street."

When we arrived at the station, I figured he'd show me a map. But instead, he walked with me—bike in hand—a block and a half.

"That's Jaffa Street. The train tracks go straight down. You can't get lost. It's about two miles to 44 Jaffa Street; it's on the left."

Obedience on Two Wheels

Of course, I didn't know it at the time, but this kind man was the first of three very different men God used to teach me lessons of obedience, faith, and trust during this trip.

Bicycle Man was OBEDIENT.

He'd ridden that train for four years without ever being redirected. But that day, God rerouted him—for me.

We took a picture together—bike and all. Then he left to check his rental properties, and I walked the rest of the way to the hostel.

Marveling at God's guidance. Amazed by His provision. Thankful for His call.

Reflection

God doesn't always give us a map—He gives us His presence. What began as a journey by faith became a living testimony of divine orchestration. From the customs counter in Germany to the bus stop in Israel, the Lord proved over and over again that obedience opens doors. Even when help didn't show up "in" the airport, it was already waiting "at" the airport. When we walk by faith and not by sight, we learn that God isn't just with us—He goes before us.

Scripture

"And thine ears shall hear a word behind thee, saying, This is the way, walk ye in it, when ye turn to the right hand, and when ye turn to the left"
—Isaiah 30:21.

Prayer

Lord, thank You for ordering every step of those who trust in You. Teach us to walk by faith—not just in big decisions but in the quiet steps of daily obedience. Remove our fear and doubt when we cannot see what's ahead. Like the Bicycle Man, make us available and willing to be used by You for someone else's miracle. Help us to recognize Your voice, follow Your promptings, and give You the glory for every open door. In Jesus' name, Amen.

CHAPTER 14

A Place Prepared

There's a peace that comes when you know you are exactly where God has called you to be—not because of anything you've done, but because of the One who ordered your steps. As I stepped onto the streets of Jerusalem in the early evening light, I knew I wasn't arriving at a random address. This wasn't just a hostel at 44 Jaffa Street—it was a place prepared. Not by human hands, but by the hand of the Lord who had been guiding me since I first said yes. From the moment I walked through the doors, I could sense it: I wasn't just checking into a room; I was stepping into divine alignment.

Looking back now, I see that every detail—every delay, every decision, every divine whisper—had brought me to this threshold. God had cleared the way. And just as Jesus once said, *"I go to prepare a place for you"* (John 14:2), I believe He had done just that for me in this earthly moment. I didn't need a plan, a reservation, or even a map. I needed faith that walks. And as I would soon discover, that faith would lead me not only to the foot of Golgotha, but also to a firsthand encounter with the empty tomb.

A Hostel on Jaffa Street

It was early evening when I finally reached the hostel at 44 Jaffa Street. The sun was just beginning to dip below the horizon, casting

114

a warm golden glow over the stone buildings of Jerusalem. I stepped through the front entrance with full confidence in my heart. I hadn't made a reservation. I hadn't called ahead. But I had been sent by God— and I believed that wherever He sends, He prepares.

I approached the front desk and asked the clerk if there was a bed available for sixteen nights. He politely informed me that their stay policy only allowed for fourteen days at a time. I smiled and said, "That's fine," and without hesitation, I paid for those fourteen days.

Looking back, I realize now that this was another example of divine favor. Though the rules said fourteen days, the Lord softened the heart of the hostel manager. As we got to know each other during my stay, he graciously allowed me to remain for the full sixteen nights. It reminded me of Proverbs 16:7, which says, *"When a man's ways please the Lord, he maketh even his enemies to be at peace with him."*

The total cost for my two-week stay—which even included a modest daily breakfast of cucumbers, tomatoes, hard-boiled eggs, toast, jelly, and pita—was under $300. In one of the world's most visited cities, that was nothing short of miraculous provision. I wasn't traveling with wealth or luxury—I was walking by faith. And true to His Word, *"my God shall supply all your need according to his riches in glory by Christ Jesus"*—Philippians 4:19.

I made my way upstairs to the sleeping quarters. It reminded me of my Army days—three bunk beds to a room, simple metal lockers, and a faded two-seater couch that looked like it had weathered years of stories. I claimed a bottom bunk and watched as the hostel worker placed a little card with my name on it at the head of the bed. At that moment, I was the only one in the room.

It felt like the Lord had set this space aside just for me—a quiet, humble place to begin what He had called me there to do.

Even though I hadn't slept since leaving Lexington, I wasn't tired. I had fasted most of the way, drinking only water and juice during the flights. But instead of feeling weak or lightheaded, I felt unusually strong—like I had been sustained by something beyond food.

"Man shall not live by bread alone, but by every word that proceedeth out of the mouth of God"
—Matthew 4:4.

I had been feasting on faith, and it was enough.

The Skull and the Tomb

Time moved differently in Israel. On that trip, I rarely ate unless the Lord directed it. Some days, I'd go without food altogether and feel completely fine. When hunger finally nudged me, I'd follow my nose to a local bakery, grab a piece of bread or pastry, and keep walking. It felt like I was living a modern-day version of Exodus 16, where the Israelites gathered manna as the Lord provided—never too much, never too little.

I set my backpack down on the bunk and felt the unmistakable pull to get moving. I stepped out of the hostel, turned left onto Jaffa Street, and began walking with no destination in mind. No map. No GPS. No agenda. Just trust. I thought about Isaiah 30:21: *"And thine ears shall hear a word behind thee, saying, This is the way, walk ye in it..."* I was walking in it—guided not by my eyes, but by His Spirit.

"The steps of a good man are ordered by the Lord: and he delighteth in his way."
—Psalm 37:23.

A few minutes into the walk, I came to a large intersection as I looked straight ahead. There, rising in ancient glory, stood the walls of Old Jerusalem. Something inside me stirred. The Spirit nudged me to turn left and continue. So, I did. With the ancient walls now to my right, I passed the Damascus Gate, crossed another street, and began making my way up a long sidewalk.

That's when I heard it—clear, internal, and unmistakable: **Stop. Look.**

I halted immediately. My eyes shifted to the left. Just beyond a line of buses parked in a nearby lot was a rocky cliff. I stepped closer and looked over the top of the buses My heart dropped. There it was.

The skull. Golgotha.

This was the symbolism of what I had seen back on the mountain in Kentucky—the skull, which was a skull-shaped rock, just as the Bible tells us. My knees went weak. I knew in that moment that this was the exact place God had shown me in a vision before ever setting foot on Israeli soil. My mouth whispered a breathless prayer: "Lord… You were preparing me for this all along."

> *"And he bearing his cross went forth into a place called the place of a skull, which is called in the Hebrew Golgotha"*
> —John 19:17.

I walked through the bus lot, drawn to the cliff like a magnet. I snapped a few pictures, but mostly I just stared. The awe was overwhelming—not the kind that shouts and dances, but the kind that brings stillness to the soul. This was holy ground. And somehow, God had brought me here the very first night.

The Eastern Gate and the Word Fulfilled

Still in awe from seeing Golgotha, I slowly walked back toward the sidewalk. My steps were careful, as if I might miss something sacred if I hurried. After just a short distance—maybe a hundred feet—I saw a narrow alleyway on my right. Something stirred in my spirit again.

Turn here. I obeyed.

The alley was quiet and straight, lined with stone walls and small shops. As I walked a short distance, my eyes locked on a sign ahead:

The Garden Tomb.

My heart leapt.

Admission was free. I stepped inside the doorway, unsure what to expect, and was greeted by friendly people whom the Spirit of God dwelled in. They offered a personal tour, but I wanted to go alone. That was no problem at all. I followed the path through a garden of peace. Flowers bloomed in bursts of color around me. Birds chirped. The city noise faded behind the stone walls. It felt like a hidden sanctuary in the middle of chaos.

Then I reached the first lookout point—an elevated terrace that overlooked the very cliff I had just seen from below. There it was again. The Place of the Skull. Now visible from above, its presence loomed as both history and prophecy fulfilled. I was standing in the very place where Jesus Christ, the Son of God, had been crucified for the sins of the world—including mine.

> *"Surely he hath borne our griefs, and carried our sorrows...*
> *But he was wounded for our transgressions, he was bruised*
> *for our iniquities..."*
>
> —Isaiah 53:4–5.

Tears filled my eyes.

I continued down the path, following the signs until I came face to face with the entrance to the empty tomb.

And I froze. This was it.

Inside, the tomb was cool and still. Cut into the rock, the empty space where His body had once been laid seemed to echo the silence of resurrection. There were no crowds, no fanfare—just the stillness of victory. Death had no voice here. Only life remained.

I whispered aloud:

"He is not here: for he is risen, as he said"
'—Matthew 28:6.

Faith had become sight. All the moments that had seemed so mysterious before—the visions, the voices, the cloud formations back home, the skull on the mountain, the phrase "Come and see the place where the Lord lay"—they all came together in that moment like pieces of a divine puzzle. I wasn't just in a place of history. I was in the middle of a story God had written for me to walk out.

Later, I told my cousin Martina what had happened.

"You saw the Skull and the Tomb your first night there?" she asked, wide-eyed.

"Yes," I replied. "The exact vision from the mountain."

I told her I had gone back so many times during my trip that the staff at the Garden Tomb started calling me 'Kentucky.' It made them smile—and reminded me how far God will go to make His presence known, even to a simple man from a small town in Kentucky.

My Restless Spirit

That evening, I didn't want to stay inside. The wonder of the day had stirred something deep in me, and I knew I needed to walk it out—literally. With no plans, no guide, and no understanding of Jerusalem's layout, I simply started walking. Every step felt directed, every corner a divine appointment waiting to unfold.

I wandered through the city, weaving between ancient walls and narrow streets as the golden hour settled over Jerusalem. The light was soft, almost reverent, like it, too, knew the holiness of the place.

Eventually, I found myself near the Eastern Gate—the very gate the prophet Ezekiel had written about:

*"Then said the LORD unto me; 'This gate shall be shut,
it shall not be opened, and no man shall enter in by it;*

because the LORD, the God of Israel, hath entered in by it, therefore it shall be shut. It is for the prince..."
—Ezekiel 44:2–3.

The gate was sealed shut with massive stones—just like the prophecy declared. It was a powerful sight. As I stood near it, I realized I was seeing, with my own eyes, evidence of God's Word fulfilled. This wasn't just a passage in the Bible. It was right in front of me—real, solid, and still waiting for its final moment when the Messiah returns to enter through it again.

There was an open security gate nearby. It had no signs in English, but I felt a nudge to walk through. **And I did.**

I stepped closer to the Eastern Gate than I ever imagined possible. From that vantage point, I could clearly distinguish between the ancient stones from Solomon's era and the later additions from Herod's time. It was a lesson in history and prophecy all at once.

But even more than the stonework, I sensed the presence of the Holy Spirit. Not in thunder, not in fire, not even in a loud voice—but in the stillness, the knowing, the peace that passes understanding.

It was humbling. I was just one man in a crowd of tourists and locals, walking around the holiest city on earth. No one knew me. No one noticed me. But God saw me. He had invited me. He said, **"Come,"** as He does to all who will listen.

And I realized something important: I didn't feel alone. I felt covered, guided, and embraced by the presence of the Lord. Just as Jesus had promised:

"I will not leave you comfortless: I will come to you"
—John 14:18.

It struck me how often people tell me, "I want what you have—I want to hear God's voice."

I always tell them, "You can." He speaks every day, but most of us aren't listening. We're too distracted. Too busy. Too self-focused.

Hearing from God requires quieting everything else, surrendering your own will, and making space for Him to speak.

As I continued walking through Jerusalem, I felt this truth rising in my spirit: the whole world could be against me, and it wouldn't matter—because God was with me.

> *"What shall we then say to these things? If God be for us, who can be against us?"*
> —Romans 8:31.

That night, by the time I returned to the hostel, I was completely overwhelmed—with gratitude, awe, and a sense of peace I had never experienced before. My first night in Jerusalem, and God had already confirmed so much. The visions, the leading, the voices, the call to "Come"—all of it was being fulfilled step by step.

And so began my stay at 44 Jaffa Street—sixteen nights in a simple bottom bunk, in a small upstairs room that would become my sanctuary during the days ahead.

Each morning at the hostel began the same way: cucumbers, tomatoes, and hard-boiled eggs were laid out at the "common area" on top of the roof. The same breakfast every day, but somehow it never felt routine. I had come to Israel with no plans and no agenda, but the Holy Spirit was laying out an itinerary of His own—one step at a time.

Some mornings, I'd leave before the sun was fully up. I had no map in my hand, no GPS, and no local guide. But I had something better—someone better. I was learning to walk by faith, not by sight (2 Corinthians 5:7). My only instructions were:

"Walk. Listen. Watch."

And He always led me as He taught me *"Obedience (Walk), Faith (Listen), and Trust (Watch)."*

One of those first mornings, I remember waking up with fresh anticipation in my heart. I stepped outside and turned right this time, heading in the opposite direction from my first evening's walk. I passed coffee shops and souvenir stands, inhaling the aroma of fresh bread and cardamom-spiced tea. The air was cool, the city just beginning to stir. But in my spirit, it felt like something had already begun. It was as though Heaven had opened a window and poured purpose into my steps.

I didn't know where I was going. But I knew He did.

Somewhere along the path that morning, I sat on a quiet stone bench and opened my Bible. I had tucked it into my backpack before leaving the hostel, and it was quickly becoming the most valuable item I carried. Every word seemed alive—sharp, specific, timely.

> *"Thy word is a lamp unto my feet, and a light unto my path"*
> —Psalm 119:105.

It wasn't just poetic. I was living it. The Word of God was actually guiding my steps in a foreign land. It wasn't telling me where I'd sleep next week or who I'd meet that day, but it was lighting my path for right now—and that was enough.

Some days, I'd get turned around and find myself walking in circles. Other times, I'd stumble upon a site I didn't even know existed—like a courtyard where someone was singing praises in Hebrew, or a rooftop with a view that stretched over the entire city. But every moment felt appointed.

There were times I sat in silence for what seemed like hours, watching the people pass by—Orthodox Jews rushing to prayer, Muslim families shopping for bread, Christian pilgrims clutching their tour books. And there I was—a man from Kentucky, standing in the middle of prophecy, feeling as if I had stepped into God's own heartbeat.

What amazed me most was the simplicity of it all. I hadn't arrived with a study group, tour group, or a mission team. I wasn't following a schedule or meeting with anyone. Yet, each day felt full—rich with revelation, brimming with the presence of God.

It reminded me of something Jesus once said:

"Come unto me, all ye that labour and are heavy laden, and I will give you rest. Take my yoke upon you, and learn of me... and ye shall find rest unto your souls"
—Matthew 11:28–29.

That's exactly what was happening. I wasn't there to impress anyone. I wasn't trying to prove my faith. I was there to learn of Him—and to find rest in the process. Not the kind of rest that comes from sleep, but the kind that settles your soul and steadies your spirit.

As the early days unfolded, the rhythm became clear: walk, listen, watch. And every time I obeyed—even in the smallest ways—I discovered more of His presence. A stranger would speak a confirming word. A breeze would stir at just the right moment. A locked door would suddenly open. The Holy Spirit was teaching me that God doesn't need our plans—He only needs our yes.

And I was learning to say yes more quickly.

It didn't matter if I ended the day with sore feet or an empty stomach. What mattered was this growing trust—this sacred dependence. Like Israel in the wilderness, I was being fed with daily manna, spiritual nourishment that came just when I needed it.

There was one day early on when I found myself standing in silence by the Western Wall. Hundreds were praying—some rocking, some weeping, some reciting scripture aloud. I stood back, unsure of what to do, when the Holy Spirit whispered gently:

"Be still, and know that I am God"
—Psalm 46:10.

I closed my eyes, let the noise fade into the background, and just stood there—still, silent, surrendered. And in that moment, I knew: I wasn't here just to see the Holy Land.

I was here because the Holy, Almighty God had invited me with one word, **"Come."**

123

Reflection

Sometimes the most profound moments come when we least expect them—when we simply say yes and follow without knowing where the path will lead. God doesn't always give the full picture ahead of time. But when we trust and obey, we discover that He has already gone before us. What may seem like coincidence is often divine orchestration. Like the skull on a mountain or a tomb in a garden, these signs of faith come alive when we walk them out.

Scripture

"Thou wilt shew me the path of life: in thy presence is fulness of joy; at thy right hand there are pleasures for evermore"

—Psalm 16:11.

Prayer

Lord, thank You for preparing the way before me, even when I don't understand where You're leading. Thank You for showing me the sacredness of surrender, the peace of obedience, and the joy of discovering Your promises fulfilled. Help me to walk by faith, to follow Your voice, and to rest in Your presence. Wherever You lead, I will go. In Jesus' name, Amen.

CHAPTER 15

Walking the Word: Sacred Stones and Divine Signs

There's something unforgettable about waking up in Jerusalem—especially when the Lord Himself stirs your soul before the sun rises. From the very beginning of this solo journey, I knew I was walking on holy ground—not only in the physical sense, but in the spiritual. Every stone I stepped on, every turn down an ancient alley, every whisper of wind through the olive trees felt soaked with the presence of God. I hadn't come to be a tourist; I had come to follow His voice. And each morning, when the Lord said, *Go,* I went. With no schedule but His, and no plan but obedience, I found myself in places I had only ever read about—walking not just through the streets of Jerusalem, but into the living Word of God.

Every morning of that first solo trip, the Lord woke me between 5 and 6 a.m.—most often right at 5. **Go,** He would say.

I would shower, shave, and quietly ease out of the room to watch the sunrise over Jerusalem. In those early hours, I explored everything my eyes could behold—the Mount of Olives, the old city gates, narrow alleys, and sacred places I had only read about in Scripture. I often carried my Bible with me so I could read the Word right where the events had taken place. It brought the Scriptures to life in a powerful

125

way. I could almost hear Jesus' voice echoing through the very stones beneath my feet. As the psalmist declared:

"Walk about Zion, and go round about her: tell the towers thereof. Mark ye well her bulwarks, consider her palaces; that ye may tell it to the generation following"
—Psalm 48:12-13

On that first full day, I woke up in awe of what God had already done. I was eager to revisit the Garden Tomb and Golgotha—and to see wherever else the Lord would lead me.

Two Tombs, One Truth

The Lord specifically directed me back to the Garden Tomb to meditate on the Resurrection. I sensed His presence so powerfully there that I returned many times during my trip to pray and read my Bible. It became my place of solitude with Jesus.

Later that evening, I walked through the winding alleys of the Old City to visit the Church of the Holy Sepulchre—a site many believe to be the traditional location of Jesus' crucifixion, burial, and resurrection. The moment I stepped through its ancient doorway, I was struck by how different the atmosphere was compared to the Garden Tomb.

Inside, pilgrims from around the world knelt, prayed, wept, and kissed the Stone of Anointing—believed to be the slab where Jesus' body was prepared for burial. Some say the slab dates back to 345 AD, others claim it is only about 200 years old. Either way, it does not reach back to the time of Jesus, according to my findings.

Incense filled the air, candles flickered on centuries-old altars, and priests in ornate robes moved about reverently. The dim lighting and echoing prayers reminded me that this place had been sacred to millions for generations.

I climbed the narrow stone stairway to the traditional site of Golgotha. There, above my head, stood a chapel built over the rock of Calvary itself. Some pilgrims knelt and reached their hands beneath the glass to touch the stone. Others simply wept. Whether or not this was the exact spot, I couldn't deny the sacred weight of what had taken place nearby—the crucifixion of the Savior of the world.

As I stood in that hallowed place, I remembered Jesus' words to the woman at the well:

> *"The hour cometh, when ye shall neither in this mountain, nor yet at Jerusalem, worship the Father... But the hour cometh, and now is, when the true worshippers shall worship the Father in spirit and in truth: for the Father seeketh such to worship him"*
>
> —John 4:21, 23

The Garden Tomb spoke to me in quiet simplicity. The Church of the Holy Sepulchre spoke through centuries of devotion. But both pointed to the same truth: the tomb is still empty. *He is not here: for he is risen, as he said.* (Matthew 28:6)

Signs Along the Way

I walked wherever the Spirit led. I didn't hear God audibly, but His voice in my thoughts was unmistakable.

At one point, I was heading toward the Western Wall to pray. The Lord reminded me:

Watch the signs.

I was in full stride, moving quickly, when His voice came again:

Where are you going?

"To the Western Wall," I replied inwardly.

Not that way. You missed a sign. I told you to watch the signs.

I was sure I hadn't missed anything. But when I retraced my steps, I realized I had taken the wrong turn. I was supposed to go the other way. Later, as I reflected, Isaiah 30:21 came alive:

And thine ears shall hear a word behind thee, saying, This is the way, walk ye in it, when ye turn to the right hand, and when ye turn to the left.

When I finally reached the Western Wall, I was struck by the devotion of those gathered. Men and women prayed separately—men to the left, women to the right. Not knowing, I tried to go pray on the women's side, and a Jewish woman sternly corrected me. I quickly apologized!

This wall was part of the ancient Temple foundation. Everything on top—the Temple itself—was destroyed in A.D. 70, just as Jesus prophesied:

"Verily I say unto you, There shall not be left here one stone upon another, that shall not be thrown down"
—Matthew 24:2

For devout Jews, this wall remains the holiest accessible site of prayer. Many come praying for the Messiah and for the Temple to be rebuilt. As I watched them cry out with such zeal, Romans 10 came to mind:

For I bear them record that they have a zeal of God, but not according to knowledge. For they being ignorant of God's righteousness, and going about to establish their own righteousness, have not submitted themselves unto the righteousness of God. For Christ is the end of the law for righteousness to every one that believeth.
—Romans 10:2–4

Day after day, I too returned to the Wall—praying to my Almighty Father through Jesus, my Mediator and Intercessor. What sweet times of prayer I had! For *"there is one God, and one mediator between God and men, the man Christ Jesus"* —1 Timothy 2:5

Encounters of Faith

Another sound I had to get used to was the Muslim call to prayer echoing over the city. At first, I had no idea what it was. Some Christians feel uneasy hearing it in the Holy Land.

But one day, a young Muslim man came to me and said, "I respect your Jesus." I hadn't spoken a word. He came to me. He could tell I was a Christian. That encounter opened my heart.

I've talked with many Muslim men, and I've always been treated with kindness. Some even called me "brother" and hugged me before parting. All people are made in the image of God (Genesis 1:27). Jesus never condemned the lost—only the prideful religious leaders who refused Him. We are not called to condemn either. We are called to love, respect, and let the Spirit speak through us so that Jesus may be seen in us. *And that he died for all...* (2 Corinthians 5:15)

A Missed Tour, A Divine Appointment

Some days in the Holy Land unfolded like a well-planned tour—and others felt like a test of faith. This was one of those days. What began as a simple schedule—get up, meet the bus, and head to Nazareth—quickly unraveled into something far deeper.

That morning, I had no idea I would meet a weary man, named Rob, walk into a divine delay, and sit above a prophetic valley that stretches across both geography and time. What looked like a missed opportunity became a moment of decision—not just for me, but for many.

"Multitudes, multitudes in the valley of decision..."
—Joel 3:14

I rose early, full of anticipation, backpack ready and heart expectant. At 5:50 a.m., I waited where the manager at the hostel had told me the tour bus would stop. The sun climbed over the rooftops. Minutes passed. No bus came. Ten minutes. Thirty. Still nothing.

Frustration crept in. I checked my ticket again. Everything seemed right—yet I had been left behind. Disappointed, I started back toward the hostel. I had longed to see Nazareth and the Sea of Galilee, but instead I wandered the streets of Jerusalem, frustrated and confused.

That's when the Lord interrupted.

What are you doing?

I froze. The voice wasn't audible, but it was clear.

"I don't know," I admitted in my spirit.

Where are you going?

I had no answer. I was simply walking in circles, lost in alleys that all looked alike.

Stop. Be still. Ask the boy.

I looked around and thought, *What boy*. At that exact moment, a young boy walked by. I hesitated, then asked, "Jaffa Street?" He repeated my words, pointed straight ahead, and kept walking.

A quiet nudge. A divine encounter. *"A little child shall lead them"* (Isaiah 11:6).

It was a WOW moment for me!

God used a boy to realign my steps, both physically and spiritually. Proverbs 3:5–6 whispered across my heart:

Trust in the Lord with all thine heart; and lean not unto thine own understanding. In all thy ways acknowledge him, and he shall direct thy paths.

Back at the hostel, the truth hit me hard: my watch was set an hour off. The tour hadn't failed me—I had failed to align with the right time. How often do we miss God's appointments because we aren't synchronized with His timing? *"To every thing there is a season, and a time to every purpose under the heaven"* (Ecclesiastes 3:1).

Rob and the Heavy Bags

Still processing the lesson, I walked into the bunk room and saw a man I'd never met sitting quietly on the sofa. The room was usually empty, but here he was—tall, with graying hair pulled back, his eyes heavy with weariness.

"Is it alright if I sit here a while?" he asked softly.

"Of course," I replied. "You paid your $14 just like I did."

He glanced at my small backpack. "Where's the rest of your stuff?"

"This is it," I smiled. "Just a Bible, a few clothes, and a whole lot of faith."

His eyes filled with tears. "The Lord told me the same thing," he said, looking down at his overstuffed bags. "But I didn't listen. I brought too much." After a pause, he added, "I came all the way from Nebraska."

His words pierced me. Spiritually and physically, I, too, had once carried too much. The Lord had called me to lay aside the unnecessary—and this man named Rob was a living reminder. Isaiah's words echoed in my heart:

> *"For my thoughts are not your thoughts, neither are your ways my ways, saith the Lord. For as the heavens are higher than the earth, so are my ways higher than your ways, and my thoughts than your thoughts"*
> —Isaiah 55:8–9

Rob didn't need a sermon. He needed a friend. We sat and talked of faith. When the housekeeper came in and wrote his name on a bunk card, he stayed seated, quietly worn. Twice, he asked if it was alright to keep sitting. Twice, I told him yes.

As I walked back into the streets, I realized—this wasn't a missed tour. This was a divine intersection. Two pilgrims, two roads, one Shepherd.

The Valley of Decision

My wandering steps eventually carried me to the edge of the Kidron Valley, lying between the Mount of Olives and the Old City. I sat in silence as the breeze stirred around me.

This was no ordinary valley. My Bible called it the Valley of Jehoshaphat—the Valley of Decision.

> *"Multitudes, multitudes in the valley of decision: for the day of the Lord is near in the valley of decision"*
> —Joel 3:14.

I looked out across the landscape and felt the weight of prophecy. This ground would one day bear witness to the gathering of nations for judgment. Then Revelation came alive in my spirit:

> *And the winepress was trodden without the city, and blood came out of the winepress, even unto the horse bridles, by the space of a thousand and six hundred furlongs.*
> —Revelation 14:20

Sixteen hundred furlongs—about 200 miles. I remembered my later drive from Jerusalem to the Red Sea: 200 miles exactly. The Word of God is precise.

(During that trip I was overcome as I passed by the Kidron River at the edge of the Dead Sea. I stopped at the Kidron River's dry bed and shouted aloud, "Oh wow, Lord! Here it is! The spot You mentioned in Your Word! Thank You for showing this to me!")

Goosebumps rose as I stood there in Jerusalem overlooking the Kidron Valley. Tears flowed. This was not symbolism. This was reality—prophecy carved into the very landscape.

Jesus' warning burned in my spirit: *"Watch therefore: for ye know not what hour your Lord doth come"*
—Matthew 24:42.

I had thought I missed a tour. In truth, God had aligned me with prophecy. He had brought me to the valley to see, to pray, to understand, and to meet Rob.

Rest in the Shepherd's Timing

As evening shadows fell, I walked slowly back through Jerusalem's quiet streets, my body tired but my soul awake.

I thought of Rob and his heavy bags. Of the boy who pointed me back to Jaffa Street. Of the Kidron Valley and the day of the Lord to come.

Every step—even the ones that felt like setbacks—was divinely purposed. I slipped beneath the thin sheet on my bunk and whispered: "Thank You, Lord, for teaching me to trust You—even when nothing makes sense."

Sleep came quickly. But my spirit remained awake.

Reflection

Sometimes what feels like a delay is God's divine redirection. A missed tour became an appointment with Rob, a child's guidance, and a prophetic vision in the Valley of Decision. God's timing is never late, never wasted. His ways are higher, His path precise.

Scripture

"Trust in the Lord with all thine heart; and lean not unto thine own understanding. In all thy ways acknowledge him, and he shall direct thy paths"

— Proverbs 3:5–6.

Prayer

Lord, thank You for reminding me that even when my plans fall apart, Yours never do. Teach me to trust Your timing, to walk by faith, and to see Your hand in what feels like delay. Align my steps with Your eternal purpose. May my life bear witness that Your Word is true, and may I be ready when You call. Amen.

CHAPTER 16

When Plans Fail, Faith Finds a Way

Some chapters in life don't begin with a sunrise—they begin with silence. The kind of silence that settles over your soul when something shifts and you can't quite explain it. That morning in Jerusalem began just like that. There was no thunder or lightning, no vision or voice from Heaven—only a hallway bathed in quiet light and a vacant bunk that whispered a deeper truth: God had moved, and I almost missed it.

In a city overflowing with history, I was about to learn that the most powerful moments don't always come from standing where Jesus once stood—they come from walking where He's still leading.

Rob Was Gone

After a quiet morning shower, I stepped softly back into the dimly lit room, careful not to disturb anyone still sleeping. As I eased the hallway door open, a warm beam of light spilled into the room and landed directly on Rob's bunk. I paused, certain I would see him stir. But when I looked closer, I realized—it wasn't Rob.

The bunk was the same: same blanket, same familiar frame. But the man lying there was someone else entirely. I blinked, half expecting him to sit up, but no—this wasn't the tall man with soft eyes and a

135

questioning spirit. This was a smaller man, bald and curled up like he'd been traveling a long time. He didn't even move as I stood there, unmoving and almost breathless.

Rob was gone.

There was no note. No goodbye. No explanation. He had simply vanished from my journey as quickly as he had entered it.

And yet, I wasn't surprised.

What I felt wasn't disappointment or confusion—it was reverence. A sacred pause in time where I knew God was confirming something far more important than any scheduled tour or carefully laid plan. Rob wasn't meant to stay. He was a messenger on assignment, a brief stop in my story meant to carry more spiritual weight than I could fully grasp in that moment.

A Living Parable

It was about faith.

He had spoken to me the day before with tears in his eyes and a hunger in his voice—not just for direction, but for God. And though he may have carried too much in his backpack, he had still come by faith. That alone made him bold. That alone made him part of the cloud of witnesses God was using to teach me how to run light and listen well.

I stood there, remembering how his overstuffed backpack bulged with everything he thought he needed—piles of clothes, extra shoes, books, snacks, even souvenirs. It was packed so tight he could hardly zip it shut. That picture has stayed with me ever since, like a living parable.

So many of us do the same thing.

We carry more than the Lord ever asked us to. We take extra provisions for what He's already promised to provide. We stuff our lives with things to help us feel prepared, when God is asking for trust instead of planning, surrender instead of control.

And suddenly, the Spirit spoke to my heart again:

"I told you to travel light for a reason."

Not just physically, but spiritually. Because when your heart is too full of your own ideas, there's no room left to receive His.

Rob's departure confirmed something I had been wrestling with since the beginning of this trip: God doesn't always give us explanations—but He always gives us encounters. And when He sends someone across your path, it may not be for long—but it will always be for a purpose.

That morning, in that small Jerusalem hostel hallway, I bowed my head quietly and whispered, "Thank You, Lord. Thank You for Rob. Thank You for the reminder to lay it all down again."

I didn't need to know where Rob went. I just needed to remember where God was leading me. And in that moment, He was leading me forward—light, obedient, and unburdened.

> *"Wherefore seeing we also are compassed about with so great a cloud of witnesses, let us lay aside every weight, and the sin which doth so easily beset us, and let us run with patience the race that is set before us"*
> —Hebrews 12:1.

The Policeman and the Plan

Determined not to miss the tour again, I checked and rechecked the time. No delays today. I slung my lightweight backpack over my shoulder, Bible tucked safely inside, and stepped out onto the narrow Jerusalem street. The early light painted the stone buildings in warm gold, and I felt a renewed sense of purpose. Whatever this day held, I knew the Lord had already gone before me.

I walked with urgency toward the bus stop, determined not to repeat the previous day's mistake. But even as I hurried, a quiet voice in my spirit reminded me: *It wasn't really a mistake at all, was it?*

Sometimes God lets you "miss" what you thought was your plan, so you won't miss His.

As I reached the street corner where the tour bus was scheduled to arrive, I stood alone beneath a small sign, the early morning light casting long shadows across the pavement. Minutes ticked by. No bus. I began to grow frustrated.

"Lord," I muttered, "let's go do something else today. I'm tired of waiting again."

Just as I turned to leave, a police car rounded the corner—lights flashing—and pulled up directly in front of me. The window rolled down, and the officer leaned out calmly.

"Need some help?"

I paused. *Alright, Lord, I hear You.* I smiled and stepped back toward the curb.

I told the officer my tour bus hadn't arrived. Without hesitation, he grabbed his radio and called the company. "I'm here with Jeffrey Cromer," he said. "You're late. When will you be here to pick him up?"

A brief silence. Then he turned to me and said, "Five minutes. Stay right here. They'll be here in five minutes."

And they were. Just like he said.

As I stepped onto the bus, I glanced out the windshield—and there he was. The same officer parked nearby, making sure I got on safely.

It was more than courtesy. It was confirmation.

God had heard me. And He had answered—not with frustration, but with favor.

Nazareth, Capernaum, and the Jordan

This time, I caught the right tour—a guided day trip north through the Galilee region. As our small group loaded into the bus, I felt a peace settle over me. I wasn't just on a tour. I was on assignment.

Our guide was informative, but it was the Lord who was truly leading my heart. Every stop wasn't just historical—it was personal. Each place carried weight because of Who had walked there, not just what had happened there.

Nazareth was our first stop.

As we explored the hillside town—its modern buildings woven between remnants of the past—I thought of the painful truth that Jesus was rejected in His own hometown. He had grown up here. Played here. Learned here. But when He began His public ministry, the people who thought they knew Him best refused to believe.

> *"Is not this Joseph's son?"*
> —Luke 4:22.

With that one sentence, they dismissed the Savior of the world.

Standing outside the Church of the Annunciation, I felt the sting of rejection—not just His, but my own. I thought of the times I had shared my testimony back home and was met with silence or skepticism. I knew what it was to feel misunderstood.... And so did Jesus.

The Shoreline and the Call

From there, we traveled to **Capernaum**, the town Jesus called home during much of His ministry. The ruins were stunning—ancient stone foundations, the black basalt synagogue, and the Sea of Galilee shimmering just beyond.

I imagined Jesus teaching there... healing the sick, casting out demons, calling fishermen to follow Him. While others listened to the guide, I slipped away and found a quiet place near the shore.

I gazed at the water and thought about those young fishermen—how they left their nets without knowing what came next.

> *"And He saith unto them, Follow Me, and I will make you fishers of men. And they straightway left their nets, and followed Him"*
> —Matthew 4:19–20.

That's what faith looks like.

They didn't know where they were going. They just knew Who they were following.

A Fresh Yes at the Jordan

Our final stop that day was the **Jordan River**. Its waters were calm, greenish, and slow-moving—not what I had pictured. But the moment I stepped into that sacred water, all expectations faded.

People were being baptized. Some sang, some wept. I stood at a distance at first, then felt the Spirit nudge me: *"You're here. Enter in."*

So I did.

I wasn't there to be saved—I had already been born again. This was something deeper. A personal surrender. A fresh yes.

The water was cold, but the fire in my spirit burned hotter than ever. With lifted hands, I whispered, "Jesus, I'm Yours. All of me. Again."

It wasn't on the itinerary.

But it was exactly what He had planned.

That evening, as the sun slipped beneath the horizon, I lay on my cot and whispered a prayer of gratitude for the day the Lord had given me. My heart was full, yet I longed for guidance. So I prayed simply:

"Lord, would You send me someone who knows Your Word— someone who could take me to places I wouldn't otherwise see here?"

With that earnest prayer, I drifted off to sleep.

Reflection

Some of God's greatest lessons come wrapped in the unexpected. When plans fall apart, divine appointments often unfold. Rob's departure, a delayed bus, a policeman's favor, and the sacred water of the Jordan all reminded me: faith doesn't follow a map—it follows a voice. A voice that says, "Come," even when we don't know where the path will lead.

Scripture

"The steps of a good man are ordered by the Lord: and He delighteth in his way"

—Psalm 37:23.

Prayer

Lord, thank You for the detours that draw me closer to You. When my plans fail, help me to trust that Your purpose remains. Teach me to lay aside every weight and follow You with a willing heart. Even when I don't see the full picture, I choose to walk by faith—not by sight. In Jesus' name, Amen.

CHAPTER 17

The Garden, the Guide, and the God Who Sends

It was still dark when I opened my eyes. The quiet hum of the hostel was all around me—distant snores, soft footsteps in the hall, a faint flicker of the streetlight peeking through the curtains. Then I heard it.

Not out loud. Not with my ears. But clearly—deep within my spirit: "Go." Just one word. Firm. Gentle. Irresistible. There was no room for confusion. I knew it was the Lord. He didn't give me a destination. No instructions. Just a divine nudge that stirred my heart awake.

Without hesitation, I got up. I showered, shaved, and dressed. Everything about that morning was quiet and purposeful, like the Lord had already set everything in motion, and I was simply catching up to His timing. There was no anxiety, no need to check a map or make a plan. I just obeyed. It was so easy...

Walking Without a Map

The front door of the hostel clicked behind me as I stepped outside into the cool morning air. The city was still stretching itself awake. The sky above Jaffa Street was a soft blend of midnight blue and the first blush of gold. The air was crisp, and the breeze carried the scent of fresh bread and stone dust.

142

I began to walk. There was no agenda. I had no idea where I was going. Only that the Lord had said, "Go." With each step down Jaffa Street, I whispered praise.

Thank You, Lord. Thank You for this day. Thank You for bringing me here.

The pavement beneath my feet felt like holy ground—not because of where I was, but because of Who I was walking with and Who I was talking to.

The Garden of Surrender

As I reached the outer walls of the Old City, I turned left, letting my feet move as the Spirit led. I passed the Damascus Gate, where centuries of history seemed to echo off the stone. I kept walking until I came to a corner, then turned right and continued.

The city was beginning to stir now—roosters crowed in the distance, shopkeepers rattled metal gates open, and sunlight spilled across the ancient stones. A gentle breeze began to blow. It was then that I looked out across the Kidron Valley and felt the pull of a sacred memory.

I haven't been to the Garden of Gethsemane yet...

That was enough. I turned in that direction and let my steps quicken. I wasn't chasing a destination—I was following a presence. God had called me to go. Now I was about to learn why.

The closer I came to the Garden of Gethsemane, the quieter everything seemed to grow—not just around me, but within me. The buzz of the city faded behind the trees. The rhythm of my footsteps slowed. It felt as though the very atmosphere had changed—as if Heaven was leaning in. This wasn't just a garden.

It was a threshold. A place of surrender.

I stood still outside the entrance for a moment, gazing at the ancient olive trees that dotted the hillside. They twisted and curved in every direction, silent witnesses to centuries of history—battles fought, prayers prayed, blood spilled, and glory revealed.

It was here, in this garden, that Jesus wrestled with the weight of His calling. It was here He told His disciples, *"Watch and pray..."* It was here they fell asleep. And it was here that He walked, alone, just a stone's throw away, and cried out to His Father:

> *"...O my Father, if this cup may not pass away from me, except I drink it, thy will be done"*
> —*Matthew 26:42.*

Olive Roots and Eternal Strength

I stepped through the gates of the Church of All Nations, which now covers the very spot where that anguished prayer was believed to be spoken. The church is both humble and majestic—a mosaic of global worship rising from the place of the world's greatest submission. I walked slowly down the aisle, breathing in the reverence of that space.

Candles flickered in the shadows. Tourists whispered softly in different languages. But I wasn't listening to them—I was listening for Him.

Jesus, what did it feel like to kneel here? To sweat drops of blood? To surrender completely, knowing what lay ahead?

I bowed my head and whispered, "Not my will, Lord, but Yours."

After a few quiet moments, I stepped back outside into the morning light and wandered next door into the olive grove. The trees stood like silent sentinels, some almost a thousand years old. I approached them with reverence, curious to know if any had stood since Jesus walked here.

I later learned that the oldest of them—carbon dated to the year 1092 AD—had likely regrown from ancient roots. Though the garden had faced sieges, fires, and destruction, the roots remained alive underground. And after every storm, they grew again.

I paused beneath one particularly ancient tree and ran my hand gently along its bark.

Maybe… just maybe… the roots beneath my feet once felt His presence. Maybe these trees wept with Him. Maybe they knew.

It was as if Jesus Himself was whispering to the deepest part of my soul…

"Jeff, you're going to be cut down. There will be seasons where you are trampled on—by disappointment, betrayal, or misunderstanding. The winds of life will knock you down. You may even feel forgotten in the soil, buried beneath the weight of what you cannot control. But hear Me: always rise. Because your roots are strong. Not because of who you are, but because of where you've planted yourself—deep in Me."

I couldn't rush this moment. I slowed my steps and prayed as I walked, thanking the Lord for the overwhelming presence of Him. There was something here—an invitation to go deeper, to listen more closely, to surrender more fully.

The Cave of Decision

I walked to the other side of the road and noticed a door with *Gethsemane* written overhead. I walked inside. It was a small cave set into the hillside, and my heart stirred. Some believe Jesus and His disciples took shelter there that night. I imagined them huddled together, uncertain of what was to come. I pictured Jesus rising from that cave, walking into the garden with Peter, James, and John… and then stepping farther into the shadows to meet with the Father, alone.

And then I understood: This was not a place of comfort. It was a place of decision. A place where the will of man was laid down, and the will of God was embraced—no matter the cost.

I stood still, barely breathing, and asked, *Lord, what else are You trying to show me?*

The answer wouldn't come all at once. It would unfold, step by step.

But I knew this much: there are places in life where we must stop walking in circles and start walking in surrender.

This was one of those places.

The Climb of Faith

Leaving the garden behind, I turned to follow the road that went up to the top of the Mount of Olives. The morning sun was now casting a gentle glow over the eastern slopes. I walked slowly, still wrapped in the silence and gravity of what I had just experienced. But the Lord wasn't finished with me yet.

A short distance ahead, I noticed a long stairway veering off to the right. It looked old and worn, yet it rose with purpose—like it was leading somewhere important. I paused for a moment, unsure. And then I felt it again. That unmistakable prompting deep in my spirit:

Take those stairs.

I looked up. The steps wound upward in layers, disappearing around bends and behind stone walls. It didn't look like a short climb. But I didn't question it. I turned and began to climb.

Step after step. Flight after flight.

I began counting, then stopped. It was pointless. The climb wasn't just physical—it was spiritual. With every step, something in me was being tested. Strength. Endurance. Trust.

After several minutes, I stopped to catch my breath and looked up—only to discover there was still more. Another turn. Another staircase. Another stretch of steps climbing farther into the sky.

Nobody's going to believe this, I thought, chuckling to myself. *This feels like a million steps!*

I pulled out my camera and started snapping photos. Maybe later, I'd use them to help tell the story. But in that moment, my legs ached, and my chest was burning. I leaned against the stone wall and whispered under my breath, "Lord... do I really need to go all the way up?"

And then He answered—not with a shout, but with certainty:

Yes. Have faith. Trust Me. I will be there.

That was enough. I kept climbing.

I realized something then: He had more faith in me than I had in Him at that moment. He believed I could make it. He knew what waited at the top. And He wanted me to experience it. So I pushed forward, one step at a time. Not because I felt strong—but because I trusted the One who had called me to climb.

Sometimes, faith doesn't feel like a giant leap. Sometimes, it just feels like the next step.

A View of Prophecy

At last, I reached the summit. And I froze in place. The moment was holy. Before me, the city of Jerusalem spread out like a golden tapestry—ancient, layered, alive. The light of the morning sun kissed its rooftops, casting shadows across temple stones and narrow streets. The Dome of the Rock shimmered in the distance, but my eyes weren't fixed on any one landmark. They were fixed on the history... the prophecy... the promise.

I stood on the Mount of Olives, where Jesus Himself had stood. This was the place of His ascension—forty days after the resurrection— when He lifted His hands, blessed His disciples, and was taken up into the clouds before their very eyes.

And this was the place where He will return.

> *"And his feet shall stand in that day upon the Mount of Olives..."*
> —*Zechariah 14:4.*

That scripture echoed in my heart as I stood on that ancient hill. The wind was still. My soul was stirred.

What if He comes back right now? While I'm standing right here?

147

I let the thought linger. I imagined Him appearing in the clouds, stepping onto the mountain, and looking directly at me. "Hello, Jeff," he'd say with a smile.

I laughed under my breath. I knew that's not exactly how it would happen, but still—it was a beautiful thought.

The Man Named Adam

Then I turned and looked across the street. A small corner market caught my eye. I instinctively reached for my camera to take a picture. But the Holy Spirit interrupted me once more:

Not here. Cross the street. Then take the picture.

It made no logical sense—but I obeyed anyway. I stepped across the street and lifted my camera.

Click.

The shutter had barely finished when I heard the sound of a car pulling up beside me. An older white sedan. The window rolled down slowly.

"Sir," the driver called out. "You're a Christian, aren't you?"

I blinked. Surprised. I wasn't holding a Bible. I didn't wear a cross. I had no shirt or sign that identified me as a believer. But somehow—he knew.

"Yes," I replied. "I am."

The man smiled widely and said words I'll never forget...

A Divine Ride

"Brother, you're not going to believe this. But, last night the Lord told me, 'Adam, clean up your car—you're going to have company tomorrow.'"

He pointed back toward the hill.

"This morning, I saw you walk past my window. And the Lord said, *'Adam, there goes the man you need to pick up.'* So, I ran into the kitchen, grabbed my keys, flew out the back door, jumped in my car... and here I am.

Where do you want to go?"

I stood there, stunned. The night before, I had prayed: *Lord, send someone who knows Your Word—someone who can take me to places I wouldn't otherwise see.*

And here he was. His name was Adam. In that moment, all the training from my military years—the caution, the warnings, the rules about strangers in foreign lands—went quiet. This wasn't a stranger. This was an answer. Without hesitation, I opened the door and got in the car.

As soon as I closed the car door, I felt a peace settle over me—a peace that surpassed understanding. I didn't know where we were going, but the Lord did. And He had already paved the way.

Bethlehem: Humility and Honor

Adam turned to me and asked, "So, where have you been so far?"

"Just Jerusalem and the Sea of Galilee area," I replied. He stared at me with wide eyes, genuinely shocked.

"You haven't seen Bethlehem? Jericho? The West Bank?"

I shook my head. "Not yet."

He smiled, leaned back in his seat, and said, "Well, brother, today is your day."

As we drove, he asked, "Do you know Brother John Hagee?"

"Yes, I do—well, not personally, but I've listened to his preaching."

Adam nodded. "He bought me this car—fourteen years ago."

I looked around the interior of the clean, worn vehicle. What seemed ordinary was actually part of a supernatural story. The Lord had provided this man a vehicle... for such a time as this.

Adam made a few phone calls as we drove. First, he reached out to a friend who was a licensed tour guide in Bethlehem. Then he contacted another friend—who owned a shop near the Church of the Nativity—and asked if he could prepare us a meal. Both of them said yes.

When we arrived in Bethlehem, I was struck by the contrast. For all its biblical significance, the town felt quiet, almost forgotten. Yet in that humble place, the Word became flesh and dwelt among us.

At the Church of the Nativity, I bowed through the small, low entrance—intentionally built that way so that everyone must lower themselves to enter. What a picture of honor and humility.

Inside, the guide led me through narrow stone passages, down into the depths of the church, where a silver star marks the traditional site of Jesus' birth. The space is adorned now with ornate materials and polished stone, but the sense of reverence remains.

I knelt silently for a moment, overwhelmed by the thought:
Here... in this town... in this very spot... He came for us.

Sacred Fellowship Around the Table

Afterward, we sat together under the fading warmth of the afternoon sun and shared a simple yet sacred meal with Adam's friend. There was no silverware, no formal place settings—just a large, worn tray set between us, piled high with the kind of food that speaks to the soul more than the stomach. Ripe figs and grapes, fresh cucumbers, warm rounds of bread torn by hand, golden olive oil shimmering in the light, and olives that tasted like they had been soaked in centuries of tradition.

We didn't just eat—we communed.

With every reach of the hand and every shared laugh, it felt as if the barriers between us melted away. We weren't strangers from different countries or faith backgrounds—we were brothers at the same table. We picked through the tray with our fingers, talking with ease, telling stories, learning names, and pausing to smile without needing to say anything at all.

It felt ancient and holy, like the kind of table Jesus Himself might have sat at with His disciples, passing bread and truth between them.

There was no performance, no pretense—just presence.

I could feel the Lord's fingerprints on every bite, every word, every glance exchanged. It was as if He had hand-prepared this moment, arranging every ingredient of the day with divine precision. The flavors were seasoned with grace. The fellowship was drenched in peace. And somewhere between the olive pits and broken bread, I realized: nothing about this day was random.

It had been written long ago, in a language only Heaven fully understands.

God was in it all—the journey, the conversation, the quiet pauses, even the laughter that echoed down the alley like a hymn.

This wasn't just a meal. It was a reminder that when you walk by faith, even a shared plate of olives can become sacred ground.

Jordan: A River of Purpose

From Bethlehem, Adam drove me to the Jordan River—the place where John the Baptist cried out in the wilderness and baptized Jesus.

As we approached the banks of the river, the landscape changed. The terrain grew flatter, more open. The water itself shimmered under the sun, flowing slowly but purposefully—just like the Spirit's leading that day.

I stood on the edge of the river in silence, imagining that holy moment when Jesus came up out of the water and the heavens opened:

> *"And lo, a voice from heaven, saying, 'This is my beloved Son, in whom I am well pleased'"*
> —Matthew 3:17.

I breathed deeply, letting the weight of that truth sink in. This was more than geography. It was destiny. And somehow, the Lord had brought me here—on a day I never planned, in a car I never expected, with a man I had just met.

Jericho: Faith That Brought the Walls Down

From Jordan, we continued to Jericho—known as the oldest city in the world, and the site of one of the most miraculous military victories in biblical history.

Adam had called ahead and had a friend waiting to walk me through ancient Jericho. As we toured the site, I couldn't help but think of Rahab, the harlot whose courageous faith changed the fate of her entire family:

"By faith the harlot Rahab perished not with them that believed not, when she had received the spies with peace"
—Hebrews 11:31.

She believed the stories she'd heard about Israel's God, and her belief moved her to action. God honored that faith—not only sparing her life, but placing her in the very lineage of Jesus.

And then there were the walls of Jericho—fortified, impenetrable, humanly impossible to breach. But God gave Joshua precise instructions:

"...Ye shall compass the city... once each day for six days. Then on the seventh day, compass it seven times, and the people shall shout with a great shout, and the wall shall fall down flat..."
—Joshua 6:2–5, 20.

I imagined the Israelites marching in silence, day after day, trusting God's strategy over their own. Then, on that final day, when the trumpets blasted and the people shouted—the walls didn't crumble backward or collapse into rubble. They fell flat.

Not one Israelite was harmed. Only God could do something like that.

As we walked through Jericho, the guide pointed out a small spring pouring out, known as Elisha's Spring. The location itself was simple—almost unremarkable—but what had happened there was anything but ordinary.

This was the very place where the prophet Elisha performed a miracle of healing—not for a person, but for the water itself.

The people of Jericho had come to Elisha with a desperate concern. The land was good, but the water was bitter. It brought death instead of life. So, Elisha took a bowl of salt, as God instructed, and declared:

> *"Thus saith the LORD, I have healed these waters; there shall not be from thence any more death or barren land"*
> —2 Kings 2:21.

And from that day forward, the waters were healed.

I stared into the spring, watching the water pour from the rocks. It still flowed—clear and clean—as it had for centuries. I was so caught up in reflection that I forgot to drink from it... but I made a mental note to come back again. (And I did later—drinking deeply from what the Lord had declared healed. It was cold, refreshing, and alive.)

I realized something: God doesn't just heal people. He heals places. He restores what's been polluted. And if He could heal water with just a word, what more could He do with a surrendered heart?

Wilderness Revelation

From Jericho, Adam and I drove deeper into the Judean Desert. The land grew more rugged and wild. Rocky hills and deep canyons stretched out on either side of the road. The terrain looked harsh, even dangerous—but something about it stirred my spirit.

As we drove, Adam pointed out various biblical sites from the window:

- The Gilboa mountain range, where King Saul fell in battle
- Remote caves where prophets once hid
- The stark beauty of the wilderness where Elijah was sustained by ravens

Then Adam slowed the car and pointed toward a steep mountain off to the right.

"Brother," he said, "I want you to climb up that mountain and look over. From the top, you'll see the St. George Monastery at Wadi Qelt—built into the cliff near the cave where Elijah stayed, drank from the brook Cherith, and was fed by ravens."

He handed me a bottle of water, smiled, and said, "I'll wait here."

I stepped out of the car and looked around. The desert was silent, except for the wind that whipped over the rocks. Off to the side of the road, I noticed a black van parked at a distance, mostly out of sight.

And that's when the enemy whispered.

Two men are waiting for you at the top. They will rob you... and throw you off the mountain.

The thought came suddenly, like a shadow trying to choke out the light. My heart skipped a beat. I stood still, staring up at the trail.

Then I answered out loud: "You ole devil, the Lord didn't bring me here to kill me." And just like that—he fled. Peace returned. Boldness filled me again. I began the climb.

The Mountain and the Men

As I reached the top, my heart pounding and my legs tired, I scanned the horizon. Sure enough—there were two men. But instead of harm, they brought help. They were kind. They spoke English fluently. And they weren't there by coincidence.

They began to tell me all about the St. George Monastery—its history, its connection to Elijah, and the prophetic significance of the site. I listened closely, knowing full well this was no random meeting.

154

Here I was—a man from Kentucky who had come all this way by faith—being driven through the Holy Land by a man named Adam, sent by God. The same man who dropped me off at the mountain and was now waiting for me in the heart of the Judean Desert... only for me to find two strangers already waiting at the top, fluent in English, ready to teach and confirm everything I'd just walked through.

What are the chances of that?

At one point, they offered to take a photo of me with the monastery in the background. I smiled and declined.

"No, thank you," I said gently. "This journey isn't about me."

They nodded in understanding. Before I turned to leave, one of them looked at me with sincerity and said,

"We would love to hear your story one day."

I smiled.

"This book... is that story."

Another divine appointment. Another confirmation that God goes before us—and meets us in the desert, just as He did with the Children of Israel during the Exodus about 3,500 years ago.

He is that same God.

Provision in the Wilderness

After the mountain descent, I climbed back into Adam's car. The wind had dried the sweat on my face, and the hike had left me exhausted—but filled.

As we drove, Adam began pointing out more significant sites:

- The Tomb of the Prophets, tucked into the slopes of the Mount of Olives
- The newly built U.S. Embassy in Jerusalem
- The sacred location of Rachel's Tomb, where Jacob's beloved wife was buried
- More sweeping views of the Judean Desert, raw and undisturbed

155

- And the solemn rise of Mount Gilboa, where King Saul took his final breath,

As the sun began to set and the roads turned back toward Jerusalem, I leaned back in the passenger seat—tired, grateful, and overwhelmed. I turned to Adam.

"Can you help me find the Upper Room?"

Without hesitation, he gave me precise directions, as if he had walked them a hundred times. Then, with brotherly care in his voice, he added,

"Brother, you've had a long, hard day. Get some rest. Go in the morning."

His words felt like more than good advice. They felt like permission. A Spirit-led pause.

As we stopped at a red light near Jaffa Street, I reached into my pocket and pulled out some folded bills—something I felt prompted to give.

"Adam," I said, "this is for your church."

He had never asked for a thing. He had paid for the fuel, made the phone calls, arranged meals, guided tours, and poured into me all day long. He had given freely, without expectation, just as a humble servant.

He looked at the offering, then looked at me. His eyes softened.

"Brother... you love to worship," he said quietly.

I was caught off guard. "What do you mean?"

He smiled, and his words cut deep—in the best way:

"I can tell by the way you give."

I had never thought of it that way before, but Adam was right. Giving... is worship.

Not just something we do out of duty. But something that reveals the posture of our heart.

"God loveth a cheerful giver."

—2 Corinthians 9:7

156

His words pierced through years of transactional thinking and unlocked a new understanding of worship—one that involved every part of life, including generosity.

The Last Adam and the Tears That Worship

As I stepped out of the car, Adam leaned across the seat one last time.

"Brother," he said gently, "thank you for your trust."

I paused, holding back tears.

"We have the same Spirit, Brother," I said.

And I meant it.

He nodded. Then he drove away.

As I made my way up the sidewalk, the weight of the day settled over me like a sacred blanket—heavy with glory, thick with wonder. My steps slowed. My heart swelled.

And then... the tears came.

Soft at first, then full and unrestrained—like a river breaking past its banks. The kind of tears that don't ask permission... they just flow.

Adam's parting words echoed in my soul:

"Brother, thank you for your trust."

But it wasn't just his voice I heard—it was as if Jesus Himself had spoken those words into the deepest part of me. And then it struck me—piercing, undeniable, holy.

His name... was Adam. The name of the first man. The name of the beginning. The name that echoes across time.

Scripture calls Jesus the Second Adam... the Last Adam—the One who came to redeem what the first had lost. A name that spans from Eden's Garden to Gethsemane's, from the fall to the resurrection, from Genesis to Revelation.

In that moment, it all collapsed into one sacred breath—Obedience, Faith, Trust.

The Lord had taught me:

- Obedience from the Bike Man at the airport,
- Faith from Rob, who disappeared,
- And now, Trust from a man named Adam, whom I freely followed because I trusted the One who sent him—Jesus, the Last Adam.

WOW.

And then, I wept.

Not just from emotion… but from revelation.

Reflection: A Journey of Obedience, Faith, and Trust

This chapter was not just a record of places visited—it was a divine unveiling of God's guidance at every turn. From a single word—*"Go"*—to a sacred climb, from an unexpected guide named Adam to ancient trees and tear-soaked prayers, every step carried prophetic weight. God wasn't just leading me through Israel; He was leading me deeper into Himself.

Each stop was more than history. It was heart surgery. Each person was more than a companion. They were confirmation. Each divine interruption was a doorway into greater trust. I didn't plan any of it.

But God did.

And in the quiet revelation that Jesus is the Last Adam, the fullness of the journey made sense. He had been with me in every whisper, every road, every step—and even in the strangers who somehow already knew me. The Holy Spirit didn't just send me. He went with me.

No tourist itinerary could've captured this day. Only the Spirit of the living God could write a story like this.

Scripture

"For as in Adam all die, even so in Christ shall all be made alive"

—1 Corinthians 15:22.

"The first man Adam was made a living soul; the last Adam was made a quickening spirit"

—1 Corinthians 15:45.

"Trust in the LORD with all thine heart; and lean not unto thine own understanding. In all thy ways acknowledge him, and he shall direct thy paths"

—Proverbs 3:5–6.

Prayer

Lord, thank You for the journey.

Thank You for the word "Go" and for the grace that meets us when we obey. Thank You for gardens that teach surrender, deserts that test our trust, and strangers who become signs of Your provision. You are the God who plans each detail, who sends us just what we need at the moment we need it.

Help me to walk by faith—even when I don't understand. Help me to trust—especially when the road is steep or the whispers of fear come. Let me hear Your voice and follow, just like I did that morning in Jerusalem.

Thank You for the man named Adam, and for the revelation of Jesus, the Last Adam. Thank You for giving me not just guidance, but presence. You are my Rock, my Root, my Redeemer—and my Friend. Let my life be a living offering. And may my obedience, my faith, and my trust bring glory to You alone. In Jesus' name, Amen.

CHAPTER 18

The Upper Room and the Birth of a Burning Hunger

The morning sun had just begun to break through the stone arches of Old Jerusalem when I stepped out, following the directions Adam had given me the day before. They led me straight to the Upper Room—tucked near the Zion Gate, not far from the ancient heart of the city.

This two-story stone structure, known as the Cenacle, is believed by many to be the place where Jesus gathered with His disciples for the Last Supper. Whether or not this was the exact location, the reverence in the air was undeniable. I stood in a place that carried the weight of remembrance—where Jesus humbled Himself to wash the disciples' feet, including Judas'... where bread was broken and wine was shared... and where the Lamb of God prepared to fulfill His purpose.

I paused, remembering how Jesus had instructed Peter and John to find the place for that sacred Passover meal. Now, after the previous day's journey filled with divine appointments, I could understand their obedience in a whole new way.

"Then came the day of unleavened bread, when the passover must be killed. And he sent Peter and John, saying, Go and prepare us the passover, that we may eat"
—Luke 22:7–8.

"Behold, when ye are entered into the city, there shall a man meet you, bearing a pitcher of water; follow him into the house where he entereth in."

—Luke 22:10

"And they went, and found as he had said unto them: and they made ready the passover"

—Luke 22:13.

As I stood within those walls, it struck me that what began as a room prepared for a meal became a place of preparation for a movement. Many Bible scholars believe this same Upper Room was the very location where the disciples gathered again in Acts 1, after Jesus ascended into Heaven. If so, this quiet chamber not only hosted the Last Supper—it became the launching place of the Church.

Waiting for the Promise

After the resurrection, Jesus didn't vanish into glory immediately. Instead, He stayed with His disciples for forty precious days—walking with them, teaching them, and proving without a shadow of doubt that He had indeed risen from the dead. The Gospels tell us He appeared to them in various places and at unexpected times, speaking of the Kingdom of God and the mission to come.

"To whom also he shewed himself alive after his passion by many infallible proofs, being seen of them forty days, and speaking of the things pertaining to the kingdom of God"

—Acts 1:3.

Before ascending into Heaven, Jesus gave one final instruction—simple, but loaded with eternal weight: "Do not leave Jerusalem." He

161

told them to stay and wait for what the Father had promised. It wasn't a suggestion. It was a divine appointment with destiny.

> *"For John truly baptized with water; but ye shall be baptized with the Holy Ghost not many days hence"*
> —Acts 1:5.

It's easy to forget that the disciples didn't know what Pentecost would look like. They weren't told exactly how long they'd be waiting, or what signs to watch for. All they had was a promise, a place, and a command to wait. So, they did.

On the 40th day, the waiting turned to wonder. From the Mount of Olives, the disciples watched as Jesus lifted His hands, blessed them, and then was taken up—carried by a cloud into Heaven.

> *"It is not for you to know the times or the seasons, which the Father hath put in his own power"*
> —Acts 1:7.

> *"But ye shall receive power, after that the Holy Ghost is come upon you: and ye shall be witnesses unto me both in Jerusalem, and in all Judaea, and in Samaria, and unto the uttermost part of the earth"*
> —Acts 1:8.

As their eyes strained toward the sky, two men in white appeared and gave them a promise that still echoes through the Church today:

> *"This same Jesus, which is taken up from you into heaven, shall so come in like manner as ye have seen him go into heaven"*
> —Acts 1:11.

They had seen Him go... and they would live—and die—with the hope of His return burning in their hearts.

In One Accord

After witnessing Jesus ascend into Heaven, the disciples didn't scatter. They didn't go back to their old lives or retreat in fear. They obeyed. They walked back into Jerusalem—back through the familiar streets, past the temple courts and crowded markets—and they made their way to the Upper Room.

There, in that sacred space, they gathered—not just the eleven remaining apostles, but others too. Mary, the mother of Jesus, was there. So were His brothers, who once doubted Him but now believed. And there were faithful women—those who had followed Jesus all the way to the cross and beyond the tomb. Together, about 120 believers waited. They didn't wait passively—they prayed.

> *"These all continued with one accord in prayer and supplication, with the women, and Mary the mother of Jesus, and with his brethren"*
>
> —Acts 1:14.

There is a certain kind of unity that can only come through shared hope. They were in one accord—one heart, one faith, one purpose. They were not only waiting for the promise of power—they were preparing for it through worship, obedience, and community.

That is exactly how "The Church" should be today.

In Unity!

The Spirit Comes at Pentecost

God's calendar is never off. His timing is precise—not a moment too early, not a second too late. While the disciples waited and prayed in the Upper Room, the streets of Jerusalem began to fill with pilgrims. Jews from every nation under Heaven were arriving to celebrate Shavuot—Pentecost—the Feast of Weeks, which occurred fifty days after Passover. What they didn't know was that God had ordained this feast not only to celebrate the wheat harvest but also to usher in a spiritual harvest that would shake the earth.

> *"And when the day of Pentecost was fully come, they were all with one accord in one place"*
> —Acts 2:1.

Fully come.

That phrase lingered in my heart as I stood in the Upper Room earlier that morning. God doesn't move until the fullness of time arrives. Just as Jesus was born at the perfect time, just as He died and rose according to the Scriptures, so now the Holy Spirit was about to be poured out—not in a vague or symbolic way, but with power, sound, and fire.

> *"And suddenly there came a sound from heaven as of a rushing mighty wind, and it filled all the house where they were sitting"*
> —Acts 2:2.

Can you imagine it? A wind not stirred by weather, but by Heaven itself. The same Spirit who hovered over the waters at creation was now filling a room with creative force again—birthing something brand new.

"And there appeared unto them cloven tongues like as of fire, and it sat upon each of them. And they were all filled with the Holy Ghost, and began to speak with other tongues, as the Spirit gave them utterance"

—Acts 2:3–4.

Not one was left out. Men, women, the timid, the bold—each one received the Holy Ghost. This wasn't a silent experience—it was loud, public, undeniable. The Spirit came not just to comfort, but to empower, to equip, and to testify.

Outside, the noise drew a crowd. People from Parthia, Mesopotamia, Egypt, Rome, and beyond gathered in amazement as they heard the disciples speaking in their own native languages.

"And how hear we every man in our own tongue, wherein we were born? …We do hear them speak in our tongues the wonderful works of God"

—Acts 2:8, 11.

It was no coincidence that these were the same languages of nations that would soon carry the gospel far and wide. God wasn't just speaking—He was sending.

Some mocked. But Peter—once the one who denied Jesus—now stood filled with the Holy Spirit, fearless and firm. He lifted his voice and began to preach, pointing to the prophet Joel:

"'And it shall come to pass in the last days,' saith God, 'I will pour out of my Spirit upon all flesh… and it shall come to pass, that whosoever shall call on the name of the Lord shall be saved.'"

—Acts 2:17, 21.

Then Peter pointed to Jesus—crucified, resurrected, exalted—and called them to repentance:

> *"Repent, and be baptized every one of you in the name of Jesus Christ for the remission of sins, and ye shall receive the gift of the Holy Ghost"*
> —Acts 2:38.

The response was staggering.

> *"Then they that gladly received his word were baptized: and the same day there were added unto them about three thousand souls*
> —Acts 2:41.

Three thousand. In one day.

The Church was born—not through marketing or strategy—but through the Spirit of the living God. What began in an upper room spread like wildfire through the streets, then the cities, then the nations. And it's still burning today.

Walking with Wonder

After spending that morning in the Upper Room, I stepped out into the sunlit streets of Jerusalem with a sense of reverence I couldn't quite explain. My footsteps were slow, deliberate. I wasn't just walking through a city—I was walking through a living story. The Upper Room had stirred something deep inside me. Not just a memory, but a hunger.

The air still held the echoes of Pentecost. I imagined the shouts of amazement, the sound of different languages blending into praise, and Peter's voice boldly proclaiming the risen Christ. As I wandered, it was as if the cobblestones whispered with history. Every turn brought me closer to the reality that this wasn't just a holy city—it was the very stage on which the Church was born.

I passed by shops and homes, arches and ancient stones, but my heart was somewhere between the past and the eternal. I tried to absorb all I could—to let it settle in my spirit like oil. I wasn't a theologian or historian by trade, but walking these streets made me hungry to know more. I didn't just want to hear the Word—I wanted to live it.

That sacred hunger—the one birthed in the Upper Room— reminded me that the same Holy Spirit who descended on those early believers now lives in every follower of Christ. That same flame still burns in hearts willing to yield. That same wind still blows through the lives of those who wait on the Lord.

> "But as it is written, Eye hath not seen, nor ear heard, neither have entered into the heart of man, the things which God hath prepared for them that love him. But God hath revealed them unto us by his Spirit..."
> —1 Corinthians 2:9–10.

Cana: The Beginning of Miracles

The tour bus wound its way through the Galilean countryside, passing olive groves and stone terraces, until we reached a quiet village nestled among the hills—Cana. I had read about this place in the Gospel of John, but now, I was standing where it happened. The site of Jesus' very first miracle. Not a dramatic healing. Not a thunderous sermon. But a quiet act of provision—turning water into wine at a wedding.

It was here that Jesus revealed His glory for the first time. Not in a temple or palace, but at a simple village celebration. I found that humbling. Our Savior chose to begin His public ministry not by making a grand political statement, but by responding to a moment of quiet crisis in a family setting. He came to serve, not to be served.

The Gospel tells us that during the wedding feast, the hosts ran out of wine—a major embarrassment in their culture. Mary, Jesus' mother, noticed and brought it to His attention.

"And when they wanted wine, the mother of Jesus saith unto him, 'They have no wine.'"
—John 2:3.

There was no panic in her voice. Just confidence. She knew something others didn't. She turned to the servants and spoke words that still echo through the centuries:

"Whatsoever he saith unto you, do it."
—John 2:5.

Those seven words pierced my heart. What if that became our life motto? What if every believer simply did whatever Jesus said?

Jesus instructed them to fill six stone jars with water. Then He told them to draw some out and present it to the master of the banquet. And when the host tasted it, he was stunned—not just by the miracle, but by the excellence.

"Every man at the beginning doth set forth good wine; and when men have well drunk, then that which is worse: but thou hast kept the good wine until now"
—John 2:10.

Jesus didn't just make wine—He made the best wine. What a picture of the nature of our Lord. He doesn't do anything halfway. He doesn't just fill—He overflows. He doesn't just redeem—He restores with excellence.

John concludes this story with a powerful statement:

> *"This beginning of miracles did Jesus in Cana of Galilee, and manifested forth his glory; and his disciples believed on him"*
>
> —John 2:11.

That miracle wasn't just about saving a wedding—it was about revealing the Messiah. It was the moment when the invisible became visible. The eternal touched the temporary. And faith awakened.

Standing in Cana, I wasn't thinking about stone jars or wine—I was thinking about obedience. Jesus could have performed that miracle without the servants. But He chose to involve them. Their obedience opened the door for a miracle.

And I thought: *Lord, help me to live that way. To listen quickly. To obey fully. To believe deeply.*

Magdala: Mary's Hometown

Our next stop brought us to the western shores of the Sea of Galilee, to a place both ancient and alive with new discoveries—Magdala. The moment our bus pulled in, I felt something shift in the atmosphere. Maybe it was the sun rising higher over the lake. Maybe it was the Spirit of God stirring something deep within. Either way, I knew this wasn't just another stop on the tour. This was holy ground.

Magdala is known as the hometown of one of the most misunderstood and deeply loved women in the Bible—Mary Magdalene. She's often associated with brokenness, yet her legacy is marked by radical transformation and unwavering devotion.

> *"...Mary called Magdalene, out of whom went seven devils..."*
>
> —Luke 8:2.

When I read that verse, I don't just see a woman who was delivered—I see the mercy of Jesus. I see what happens when the Savior steps into the chaos of a soul and speaks peace. Mary's encounter with Jesus wasn't a polite religious moment. It was a complete and total rescue.

And here I was, standing in her hometown—where her pain may have begun, but where her healing story also took root. I couldn't help but wonder... how many people in this village watched her transformation and were forever changed by it?

As we walked the grounds, our guide pointed out the ancient ruins of a synagogue discovered in 2009. It's one of the oldest ever found in Galilee, and most scholars agree it was active during Jesus' time.

"The coin we found was minted in Tiberias in AD 29," our guide explained. "That means this synagogue was here when Jesus ministered in this region."

I stood still, taking it in. The stones beneath my feet may have echoed with His footsteps. The same synagogue where He may have taught... and healed... and called people into the Kingdom.

> *"And Jesus went about all Galilee, teaching in their synagogues, and preaching the gospel of the kingdom, and healing all manner of sickness and all manner of disease among the people."*
> —Matthew 4:23

It's likely—very likely—that Jesus stood right there. That Mary Magdalene heard His voice in her own village. And what she heard didn't just stir her heart—it changed her life. She followed Him from that day forward.

Luke tells us that Mary, along with other women like Joanna and Susanna, helped support Jesus' ministry.

> *"...which ministered unto him of their substance."*
> —Luke 8:3

That may not sound extraordinary, but in first-century culture, it was. Mary didn't just follow Jesus—she gave everything to serve Him. She was there at the cross when others fled. She was there at the tomb. And she was the first to see the risen Lord.

From seven devils to the first witness of the Resurrection—what a testimony.

What a picture of grace.

As I stood in Magdala, I prayed quietly: *Lord, make me that faithful. Let nothing—no past failure or present fear—keep me from following You all the way.*

Mary was from Magdala, a fishing village on the western shore of the Sea of Galilee. The Bible calls her *Mary Magdalene*—but "Magdalene" is not a last name. It simply means *Mary, the Magdalene*, or *Mary of Magdala*. This title tied her identity not to her past failures but to the place where Jesus found her, healed her, and transformed her life forever.

What a reminder that God knows us fully—our name, our story, and even the ground we come from. Yet when He redeems us, He writes a testimony so powerful that our identity is forever linked, not to our brokenness, but to His mercy.

Reflection

The Upper Room, Cana, and Magdala each echo a part of our spiritual journey—waiting, obedience, transformation. In the waiting, we are filled. In obedience, we are used. In transformation, we become witnesses of the resurrection life.

Are we waiting in one accord for a fresh move of the Spirit? Are we ready to do whatever He says, even when we don't understand? Are we willing to follow Jesus beyond deliverance into a life of faithful service?

Like those in the Upper Room, may we wait with expectation. Like the servants in Cana, may we obey without hesitation. And like Mary of Magdala, may we follow Jesus all the way—through the cross, to the tomb, and into the glory of resurrection power.

Scripture

"Not by might, nor by power, but by my spirit, saith the Lord of hosts"

—Zechariah 4:6.

Prayer

Father, thank You for the fire that fell in the Upper Room and the Spirit who still fills us today. Thank You for the miracles at Cana that remind us You care about the details, and for the restoration of Mary that assures us no one is too far gone.

Stir up a holy hunger in us—one that won't settle for anything less than Your presence. May we be obedient servants, transformed worshipers, and bold witnesses for Christ. In Jesus' name, Amen.

CHAPTER 19

Transformed in the Fire: Lessons from the Lanes of Jerusalem

Sometimes the greatest lessons come in moments you never planned. They find you in the winding alleys of an ancient city, in the hush of a hostel bunkroom, in the unexpected brush of danger, or the whisper of a midnight prayer. This chapter is a collection of such moments—scattered, unplanned, and unforgettable.

What began as a journey by faith had become a walk of revelation, correction, and divine protection. From a street-side setup that turned into a miracle, to the hush of a whirlwind at the Western Wall, I began to realize that the same God who called me was now shaping me—refining me like gold in the fire of Jerusalem.

A Setup and a Deliverance

One quiet afternoon, I found myself wandering the maze-like alleyways of Old Jerusalem, unsure of where I was going. The ancient city has a way of turning even the most determined traveler around—its narrow paths twisting through stone walls and archways, each one looking more familiar than the last.

As I tried to reorient myself, a man called out from a small shop tucked into a corner.

"Come, my friend! Come have some tea!"

It felt harmless enough. I stepped inside, and he motioned for me to sit down. The shop was crowded with shelves full of spices, trinkets, scarves, and other souvenirs. As he poured a cup of tea, he began gathering items—small gifts, he said, for me and my wife.

"These are for you... free!" he said with a smile. "Take something home for your beautiful wife. Here, some spice too."

But something didn't sit right in my spirit. I wasn't there to buy anything. I hadn't asked for gifts, and I had no interest in collecting trinkets. Then I noticed them—several older men lingering just outside the shop, watching through the window, grinning, whispering. Their eyes weren't kind.

That's when the Holy Spirit stirred within me.

"Get up and walk out."

It was clear, unmistakable. I took one final sip of tea, stood slowly, and walked out of the shop.

That's when everything shifted. The man's smile vanished. He rushed toward me, grabbed hold of my arm and spun me around, and demanded, "Seventy-five American dollars!"

I didn't hesitate. I looked him straight in the eye and said with boldness—not from myself, but from the Spirit within me—

"Take your hands off me!"

Instantly, the man gasped for breath and let go. His face twisted in shock and confusion as he stumbled backward. I didn't say another word. I walked out and began silently counting down in awe:

Fifteen... fourteen... thirteen... all the way to zero.

God had defended me. Just like He promised. I thought back to what I had told the women at the courthouse days earlier:

If any man lays his hands on me, I believe the Lord will take his breath away.

The Word says:

"Touch not mine anointed, and do my prophets no harm"
—Psalm 105:15.

I had experienced it firsthand.

Precise Prayers and a Gentle Lesson

That night, back at the hostel, I found myself in a shared room with several other travelers. Everything was quiet—until one man's snoring erupted like a freight train. It wasn't the kind of snoring you sleep through. It sounded like a semi-truck shifting gears uphill through a tunnel, dragging its load behind it. The walls seemed to vibrate.

At first, I pulled the covers over my head and tried to ignore it. Then I laughed to myself and whispered a simple prayer:

"Lord, would You please open up that man's airway, so he won't snore that much?"

I didn't even finish the thought before the snoring completely stopped. The silence was instant and almost too perfect. I smiled in the dark, amazed again at how quickly God hears our prayers.

But two minutes later, the snoring resumed—only this time, it was softer. Instead of the sonic boom I'd heard earlier, it sounded more like a muffled purr or a gentle snuffle. Still present, but much easier to ignore.

I softly said to the Lord, "Lord, I sure thought You had stopped that man from snoring."

That's when the Lord spoke gently to my heart.

"Be precise when you pray."

It struck me. I had asked that he wouldn't snore *that much*. And that's exactly what God did. He honored the words I spoke—down to the letter.

It reminded me of the words of Jesus:

> *"What things soever ye desire, when ye pray, believe that ye receive them, and ye shall have them."*
>
> —Mark 11:24

175

And again:

"Ye have not, because ye ask not. Ye ask, and receive not, because ye ask amiss…"

—James 4:2–3.

I learned a powerful truth that night. God isn't just listening—He's responding with precision. And often, the difference between a partially answered prayer and a fully answered one comes down to the clarity and faith with which we ask.

From that moment forward, I resolved to pray more intentionally—not just casually throwing words Heavenward, but speaking with faith and accuracy, knowing my Father listens closely.

The Western Wall Whirlwind

Nearly every morning in Jerusalem, I walked to the Western Wall—also known as the Wailing Wall. It's the closest place Jews can access to where the Holy of Holies once stood, and it remains one of the holiest sites in all of Israel. I usually arrived early to beat the heat, finding quiet moments before the crowds arrived. Some mornings, I stayed 30 minutes. Other times, over an hour. There was just something about that place that pulled me into deeper prayer.

One particular morning, I made my way through the security checkpoint, touched the ancient stones, and found an open spot near the base of the Wall. I pressed my hands gently against it and bowed my head. I began to pray—not with a long list of requests, but with simple words of worship, thanksgiving, and surrender. And in that moment, something supernatural happened.

I felt it.

It wasn't a breeze, and it wasn't the heat. It was like standing in the middle of a whirlwind—not chaotic, but holy. A swirling presence surrounded me. It wasn't visible, but it was tangible. I was wrapped in something divine, and yet completely at peace.

Tears welled up in my eyes. A deep joy filled my chest. A quiet awe settled on my shoulders.

I didn't say a word. I just stood there in the whirlwind of His presence.

"Then the Lord answered Job out of the whirlwind…"
—Job 38:1.

I don't know how long I stayed there. But when the moment lifted, and the spiritual wind ceased, I stepped back—reverently, as the Jewish custom teaches—never turning my back to the Wall. I turned to leave, and only then noticed that several men had been watching me.

Their eyes were wide. Their faces serious.

What I thought had been a private encounter between me and Jesus had clearly touched others as well. I don't know what they saw or felt—but they saw something. Perhaps, for a brief moment, the curtain between the physical and the spiritual had been pulled back. Perhaps, like those on the Day of Pentecost, they sensed the nearness of something divine.

"And it shall come to pass in the last days, saith God, I will pour out of my Spirit upon all flesh…"
—Acts 2:17.

I walked away slowly, trembling a bit inside. Not with fear, but with holy reverence.

Jesus had revealed Himself to me that morning—and maybe even to others. And if He did it there, in that sacred place, He could do it anywhere. Even now. Even in the lives of those who don't yet believe.

He's done it before.

And He's not finished.

A Walk Through Prophecy

One warm afternoon, I took another long walk through the city—this time heading toward the southern end of the Old City. My steps felt unhurried, almost guided. I hadn't planned a route, but I wasn't lost either. I simply followed the nudge of the Holy Spirit, trusting He had something to show me.

Eventually, I found myself near the site of the Pool of Siloam. To my surprise, a group of archaeologists was actively working there—helmets on, tools in hand, brush and dirt swirling in the hot Jerusalem air. I paused to watch them, marveling at the ancient stone steps being uncovered. These weren't just artifacts from history—they were footsteps from Scripture being unearthed right before my eyes.

"Go, wash in the pool of Siloam..."—John 9:7.

That's what Jesus had told the blind man. And here I was, looking at the very steps that man might have climbed down before receiving his sight. The Pool of Siloam, fed by the Gihon Spring, was the water source King Hezekiah had redirected through an underground tunnel during the Assyrian threat.

> *"And he made a pool, and a conduit, and brought water into the city..."*
>
> —2 Kings 20:20.

On a later trip, I even saw a large excavator sitting right in the middle of the Pool site. The spring had been temporarily diverted, and the plan was clear: restore the ancient flow. God is still uncovering things—restoring His Word, rerouting the Living Water into places that had long been buried or blocked.

A Glimpse into the Future

After leaving the Pool, I turned into the Jewish Quarter and followed a narrow stone street called Misgav Ladach. It was there I saw a sign that made my heart leap: **The Temple Institute**.

I froze for a second. Could this really be it?

I had heard of this place years earlier—how a group of devout Jews was actively preparing for the rebuilding of the Third Temple. But now I was standing outside its entrance.

I stepped in and bought a ticket without hesitation. I wasn't just entering a museum—I was stepping into prophecy, yet to be fulfilled.

As I walked through the Temple Institute Museum, a reverent hush settled over me. This wasn't like any museum I'd ever visited. It wasn't focused on the past—it was alive with anticipation for the future. The displays weren't mere replicas or historical relics—they were functional, Temple-ready instruments built according to the specifications of Scripture.

Every item I saw—the golden menorah, the silver trumpets, the garments for the High Priest—had been crafted with stunning precision. These weren't props. They were vessels of purpose, prepared for worship in a Temple not yet rebuilt... but expected.

I stood before a scale model of the future Temple complex, stunned by the attention to detail. Every measurement aligned with the biblical pattern given in Exodus, Leviticus, and Ezekiel.

> *"And see to it that you make them according to the pattern which was shown you on the mountain"*
> —Exodus 25:40.

The museum's mission is to rebuild the Third Temple on the Temple Mount.

I could feel my spirit stirring. This wasn't about tradition—it was about preparation. I remembered how Jesus prophesied in Matthew 24 about the abomination of desolation standing in the holy place. Paul wrote to the Thessalonians that the man of lawlessness would one day exalt himself in the Temple of God.

> *"…so that he as God sitteth in the temple of God, shewing himself that he is God"*
>
> —2 Thessalonians 2:4.

Could it really be that this generation would live to see these prophecies fulfilled?

My eyes scanned the menorah, the priestly garments, the altars, the tables—all made and ready for a Temple not yet standing. I stood there, stunned. These weren't symbolic gestures. These were declarations of intent.

God was letting me peek through a prophetic window into Israel's future.

And the view was breathtaking.

Beneath the Mount

The following day, I joined a guided tour beneath the Temple Mount—an experience unlike any other. As we moved quietly through the narrow stone tunnels, I felt like I was walking through the layers of biblical history itself. Every wall, every carved stone seemed to whisper stories of kings and prophets, priests and pilgrims.

Our guide explained that these tunnels run alongside the massive foundation stones of the ancient Temple. Some of the stones we passed were enormous—measuring over 40 feet long and weighing hundreds of tons. These were not modern marvels; they were remnants of Herod's Temple, which once stood in glorious splendor until its destruction in A.D. 70, just as Jesus had foretold:

"Seest thou these great buildings? There shall not be left one stone upon another, that shall not be thrown down"
—Mark 13:2.

As we continued through the subterranean corridors, our guide pointed out a particular spot—directly across from the Holy of Holies, according to the best calculations of ancient Temple layout. Here, some devout Jews quietly gather to pray. Since they're not permitted to pray openly on the Temple Mount above, this hidden place has become their sacred sanctuary.

The tension surrounding the Temple Mount was something I had sensed in the atmosphere since my arrival in Jerusalem. Though Israel technically controls the land, a Jordanian-backed Islamic trust—the Jerusalem Islamic Waqf—maintains religious authority over the site. The golden Dome of the Rock now stands where the Temple once stood. Nearby, the Al-Aqsa Mosque welcomes Muslim worshippers daily, but non-Muslims are forbidden from praying aloud or visibly worshiping there.

It's a complicated arrangement—one layered with centuries of conflict, theology, and politics. Yet beneath it all, devout Jews still wait. Still hope. Still pray. Their hearts burn with the promise of restoration.

"Even them will I bring to my holy mountain, and make them joyful in my house of prayer… for mine house shall be called an house of prayer for all people"
—Isaiah 56:7.

Standing underground, surrounded by silence and stone, I sensed that same hope rising in my spirit. Though much remains hidden and uncertain, God's promises are never void. One day, the Third Temple will rise. One day, worship will be restored. And one day, the true King—the Messiah—will reign from Jerusalem.

As I Packed My Backpack

That final night in Jerusalem, I sat on the edge of my bunk, quietly packing my backpack. Yet a weight rested on me—a reluctance to leave, not because I didn't want to see my family, but because I had been forever changed by what I had just lived.

This wasn't a trip—it was a divine unfolding.

I had walked where Jesus walked. I had stood in sacred places. I had met people whose paths were divinely woven into mine. God had guided my steps, answered my prayers, and revealed His presence in ways I still couldn't fully comprehend.

Tears welled up as I looked around that simple hostel room. I had arrived hungry for more of God—and I was leaving full, transformed. No longer just a pilgrim. Now, a son changed by holy encounter.

I whispered like Jacob at Bethel:

"Surely the Lord is in this place; and I knew it not"
—Genesis 28:16.

And just like Jacob, I wasn't leaving the same.

Back on Kentucky Soil

After flights from Tel Aviv to Germany, then Chicago to Lexington, I stepped onto familiar Kentucky ground. But everything felt different. The landscape hadn't changed—but I had.

Throughout the journey home, my heart overflowed with gratitude. Not even layovers could frustrate me. I was still basking in His goodness.

At Bluegrass Airport, there they were—Anissa, John, and Bethany—waiting with wide smiles and open arms. I wore my old Ford Brothers cap, the same one I had before I left. But as I approached, something strange happened.

Anissa didn't recognize me at first. Bethany nudged her, "There he is, Mom."

She looked again, eyes wide. "Honey... you've changed."

She was right. It wasn't just the 40 pounds I'd lost walking miles through Israel. It wasn't the sun-weathered skin or the leaner frame. It was something deeper—something eternal. I had been pressed, refined, and filled.

> *"But we all, with open face beholding as in a glass the glory of the Lord, are changed into the same image from glory to glory..."*
>
> —2 Corinthians 3:18.

I had beheld His glory—and I was changed.

Reflection

There are places in life where God refines us—not just in theory, but in reality. Jerusalem was that furnace for me. I entered the Holy City as a pilgrim with faith, but I left as a man forever changed—pressed in spirit, purified through trials, and awakened to the nearness of prophecy. The winding lanes, the Western Wall, the silence beneath the Mount, the whisper in the Kidron Valley—all of it was His voice calling, correcting, comforting, and commissioning. God didn't just meet me there; He transformed me there.

Sometimes we don't realize how much we've changed until we come back home—and others see it too. When my wife looked at me and said, "You have changed," she didn't just see a lighter frame. She saw that the fire of God had done something within me. And the same God who walked with me in Jerusalem now walks with me here. Refined, revived, and ready to testify.

Scripture

> *"Beloved, think it not strange concerning the fiery trial which is to try you, as though some strange thing happened unto you: But rejoice, inasmuch as ye are partakers of Christ's sufferings; that, when his glory shall be revealed, ye may be glad also with exceeding joy"*
> —1 Peter 4:12–13.

Prayer

Lord, thank You for meeting me in the fire. Thank You for every moment You protected, provided, and proved Yourself faithful. Thank You for the people You sent, the places You led me, and the Word You made alive. Burn away everything in me that's not from You. Let the fire of Your Spirit continue to refine me, even when I'm far from Jerusalem. Help me walk in boldness, humility, and testimony—not because of what I've done, but because of what You've done in me. In Jesus' name, Amen.

CHAPTER 20

The Way of the Stepping Stones: 33 Days of Obedience

Some journeys don't begin with a packed bag or a plane ticket—they begin with a warning. A whisper from God. A flat tire. A sudden clarity that shakes you deeper than any sermon. That's how this one began.

I thought I was just driving to church with my daughter that Sunday morning. I didn't realize I was also driving straight into a divine redirection. A sharp rock, a slow leak, and a word from the Lord that pierced my spirit like a trumpet blast: *"Keep this truck, and you will take your last breath in it."*

Obedience is rarely convenient. It often costs us something we thought we needed. But I've learned—when God speaks, even through the hiss of a tire or the price tag on a truck, the only safe response is surrender.

What followed was a series of divine confirmations, starting with a dealership offer of exactly $33,000—the number I had prayed for. It wasn't just a sale. It was a signpost. Jesus was crucified at 33. The Sea of Galilee's circumference is 33 miles. And soon I would walk around it for 33 days, not with a plan, but with a promise.

I didn't know the route. But I knew the Guide.

And so began the next chapter of my journey—one step of obedience at a time, led by the whispers from Heaven, the markers of divine

185

appointment, and the steady hand of the One who never fails to make a way.

A Punctured Tire and a Prophetic Warning

One Sunday morning, a couple of months later, my daughter and I were on our way to church. We stopped by the office before heading on. She had recently gotten her driver's license and asked if she could drive us that morning.

"Yes, my dear," I replied, and off we went.

As she turned into the church's long gravel driveway, a sharp rock sticking straight up caught my eye. Of all the rocks in that driveway, I knew this one would puncture the tire—and sure enough, it did. The pressure gauge in the truck showed the air quickly draining from the front passenger tire. I told Bethany to get parked as quickly as possible.

At that exact moment, as the air hissed from the tire, the Lord gave me a clear and weighty thought: *"Keep this truck and you will take your last breath in it."* Just two days earlier, I had received a recall notice for the truck. I'd already scheduled an appointment with the dealership. My good friend Gary was stopping by to pick it up.

The $33,000 Confirmation

When Monday came, I sat at the office waiting for Gary to arrive. I couldn't stop thinking about the Lord's warning. I had just purchased this truck and invested a significant amount of money into it. But I prayed, *"Lord, I don't care about the money. I know I'll lose several thousand dollars, but I believe a fair price would be $33,000."* That was the number I felt impressed to settle on.

Gary arrived to pick up the truck. Later that afternoon, he called to say the dealership had it ready. I asked him to see if they would make an offer to buy it. He was surprised I'd even consider selling, but I just told him, "Well, I may be heading back to Israel again..." Moments later, Gary called back.

"Jeff," he said, "the dealership will give you $33,000 for the truck."

Without hesitation, I said, "Sold." I took the loss and obeyed what the Lord had placed on my heart.

That number—33—suddenly carried great significance. I began seeking the Lord about what to do next. Jesus was 33 years old when He was crucified. Was I supposed to go back to Jerusalem? As I researched, I discovered something astonishing: the circumference of the Sea of Galilee is 33 miles. That was it! I knew in my spirit that I was to go back to Israel and spend 33 full days at the Sea of Galilee.

Back to the Galilee—By Faith Again

This was in November 2019. I looked at the calendar and marked the dates: November 5 through December 9. I bought my plane ticket and asked the Lord once again to give my wife peace about this journey—especially since I'd miss Thanksgiving, a holiday she deeply cherished.

I told the Lord, *"If she doesn't have peace when I tell her, I won't go. I want this to be You—not me."*

When I finally shared my plans with her, she responded, "Honey, I understand. Do what the Lord is leading you to do." WOW.

At this point, I had about two weeks to prepare. I packed my backpack once again. This time, however, I rented a phone online that I could pick up at the Tel Aviv Airport.

A Journey Without Directions

I knew I was going to the Sea of Galilee—but had no idea how I'd get there. Renting a car didn't feel right. A taxi was too expensive, and I didn't feel led to take a bus from the airport either. I remembered hearing something about a train from the airport during my previous visit.

I landed in Tel Aviv around 3:30 p.m., picked up the rental phone, and made my way to the basement to buy a train ticket to Haifa. But I didn't know which stop was mine. By 4:30 p.m., it was completely dark. I was riding a train into the unknown, asking the Lord for His peace and guidance.

Signposts from Heaven

A young man sat across from me, his eyes curious, his spirit open. As the wheels of the train hummed beneath us, I began to share my story—of faith, of calling, of walking with Jesus. He leaned in, captivated. His scheduled stop came and went, but he stayed right there, caught in the moment. Neither of us noticed the time. We were both swept into something deeper than conversation—a divine appointment in motion.

He missed his stop, but he didn't seem to mind. And I... I wasn't sure where I was anymore. I wasn't from around there, and honestly, I didn't want to get lost. Quietly, I turned to the Lord in my heart and said, *"Unless someone announces Haifa, I'll just stay on this train."* Not more than a breath later, the intercom crackled—"Haifa."

I looked up, stunned, heart swelling. The voice didn't just say a city's name... it was God's whisper through a speaker, reminding me that He was guiding every step, even through the sound of a train's destination call.

I got off, saw a bus station nearby, and asked about a bus to Tiberias. A man pointed to a bus just as the door was closing. I rushed aboard and asked the Lord again for confirmation. At that moment, a car passed the bus with "33" on its license plate.

Later that evening, I was dropped off at another station—a place that looked more like a military base than a bus terminal. Concrete. Quiet. Alert. Soldiers walking around with their weapons hanging from their shoulders. I felt like a stranger in a land I didn't yet understand. I looked around, a little unsure, and asked someone about the next bus. Without hesitation, they pointed to one that was just about to pull away.

Once again—just in time.

I climbed aboard, breath catching in awe. It felt like every moment was being choreographed by unseen hands. As the bus rolled forward, winding through the dark curves of the road toward Tiberias, my eyes caught something that stole my breath.

There it was—a small city glowing like a lantern in the night, perched high above the darkness. It looked like it was suspended between Earth and Heaven.

And just like that, a verse from deep within came rushing to the surface of my soul:

> "Ye are the light of the world. A city that is set on a hill cannot be hid"
>
> —Matthew 5:14

In that sacred moment, I knew—God was not only leading my path, but He was also confirming it. Every step, every bus, every curve in the road—even the number "33" flashing by on the highway again—was His way of whispering,

"You are right where I want you."

Divine Appointments from Iran

After stepping off the bus in Tiberias, I stood there with no map, no plans—just a quiet conviction in my heart: *Go down to the Sea of Galilee.* Even though the sky was already cloaked in night, I obeyed.

I walked slowly, guided only by the rhythm of my steps and the gentle pull of the Spirit. As I drew near, the stillness of the water greeted me. The breeze off the Sea wrapped around me like a familiar blanket. The waves rolled gently onto the shore, whispering as if they remembered Him—the One who had once walked upon their surface.

It was quiet. Holy quiet.

I stood there and breathed deep. I felt at home. Peace like a river flowed through me.

I whispered, *"Lord... is this where I stay?"*

There was no audible voice, but the Lord impressed on my heart: *"Walk through the town."*

So I did.

Though it was dark, I moved through the streets of Tiberias with open eyes and a listening heart. I noticed the shopkeepers, the children, and the older men talking in groups. I heard their voices rise and fall in a language I didn't understand, yet I listened as if I did. Every step felt purposeful. Every face seemed woven into the tapestry of this divine journey.

And then—I saw it.

The hostel.

Tucked near the end of the road, as if waiting for me. I knew the moment I saw it—this was the place prepared for me.

Inside, I met a young man from Iran. He shared the room. His family had fled persecution, and he now lived in Germany.

We connected like brothers who had known each other for years, not hours. There was no barrier between us—only grace.

The next day, we visited Safed and hiked the Mount of Beatitudes with two other young men we had met on our journey. As we climbed that sacred hill, I looked at them and felt something stir in me. I wasn't just another traveler. I felt like a father among sons. Protective. Watchful. Full of wonder at what God was doing.

I began to ask quietly in my spirit: *"Lord... what are You showing me with all these divine connections?"* And though the answer didn't come in full, I knew one thing for sure: I was walking in something bigger than myself.

Stepping Stones in the Mud: A Journey to the Springs

That night, as I sat in quiet reflection, my thoughts turned to the springs that feed the Jordan River. A desire stirred in my heart—to find some of the springs that form the Jordan or that flow directly into the Sea of Galilee and dip my toes in each of them. But I had no idea where they were. I only knew they flowed from the north, somewhere off Mount Hermon.

Yet even in the unknown, I held onto one truth: God gives His children the desires of their hearts. And this was my desire. What I didn't know was that God would not only grant it—He would also exceed it, and teach me with every step I took.

The next morning, I packed up and boarded a bus, headed toward the Golan Heights. I stopped at little roadside stations that seemed to be in the middle of nowhere, waiting for the next bus to come, trusting that each one would carry me a little farther north. I had no destination in mind—only direction.

Eventually, I got off the bus in a place I didn't know existed: a town called Katzrin. As I began to walk through this beautiful town, I was taken in by the calm, the colors, and the peace that rested over it like a soft blanket. I didn't see any place to stay. But I kept walking. Then, there it was—what looked like an ordinary house turned into a hostel. And sure enough, it was.

Inside, I met a bearded young man—the hostel owner. It was late, and he was about to leave for the night. But I had just arrived. He looked at me and said, "Hello." I responded. He asked where I was from, and I said, "Kentucky." He paused, smiled, and said, "How in the world did you get here?" In that moment, I knew—I was right where I was supposed to be.

The hostel owner told me about trails that led to a spring. I set out early, walking alone. Eventually, I came to a fork in the trail and wasn't sure which way to go. And then—out of nowhere—a colt approached me and nudged me down a particular path. Yes, a colt. God sent a colt.

That trail led to a muddy stretch. I had only one pair of shoes. Looking for a cleaner route, I took another path that looked better—but it was a trap. My feet sank past my ankles. As I stood there frustrated, I heard the Lord whisper, *"Don't turn back now. Keep going."* I obeyed.

When I finally got around the mess, I looked back to the place I had been led to originally. There were stepping stones. I had passed up the path God had prepared for me and chosen the one that looked easier. Does that sound familiar?

Eventually, I reached a crystal-clear pool fed by a spring. I felt like the prodigal son. I washed my shoes and socks and rested. In about an hour, they were dry.

But the journey wasn't over.

Soon, I faced another obstacle: the trail ended at a cliff. I tried to swing around a boulder—but had no grip. I heard again, *"You've come too far to turn back."* Then: *"Let go."* I had to release what I was clinging to, without seeing what was next. I let go in faith—and instantly found a stronghold. I couldn't see it before, but it had always been there. And if the ground had given way, it wouldn't have mattered—I was holding onto my Stronghold.

The path continued beside the flowing water, and it grew deeper: ankle deep, knee deep, waist deep—then, waters to swim in. At the top, I found a breathtaking waterfall. The Lord whispered, *"How much of the Holy Spirit do you want? Ankle deep? Knee deep? Waist deep? Or waters to swim in?"*

It reminded me of the prophet's vision in Ezekiel:

> *"Afterward he measured... the waters were to the ankles... to the knees... to the loins... waters to swim in, a river that could not be passed over"*
>
> —Ezekiel 47:3–5.

That waterfall wasn't just beautiful—it was a symbol of God's Spirit being poured out, not in drops, but in floods. God desires to bless His people!

As I prepared to descend the mountain, I noticed my water bottle. Just a few sips remained. I looked up to the brilliant blue sky and said, "Lord, You brought me here—I know You'll make a way for me to get back."

As I looked down to take my first step, there he was—a young man walking up the trail toward me. He looked at my bottle and said, "You need more water." I tried to politely decline, but he insisted, "I have plenty. I have more from where that came from."

He filled my bottle, and as he handed it back, some younger children caught up with him. He was their teacher.

Does this all sound familiar?

We gathered there for a few minutes, exchanging names and stories. They were shocked to learn I was from Kentucky—and traveling alone. Or so they thought.

On the way back, I whispered, "Lord, I'll take the path You showed me first." I returned to that muddy stretch—and this time, I saw the stepping stones. They had always been there. One careful step at a time, I crossed—I was clean.

God had made a way.

The Trail That Taught Me

As I descended the mountain that day, water bottle full and heart overflowing, I realized something profound—this wasn't just a hike through the hills of Israel. It was a walk through the classroom of the Holy Spirit. Every twist in the trail, every muddy step, every whisper of wind had been ordained to teach me something deeper.

Here, in the solitude of God's creation and the stillness of His presence, I learned that faith doesn't grow strongest in the sanctuary—but in the struggle. Obedience isn't shaped on the mountaintop—it's proven on the path.

These are the ten lessons the Lord wrote into my heart:

Ten Lessons from the Mountain

1. When no one else is around, there is still One who hears you.

His name is Jesus. "Call upon Me and I will answer."

> *Scripture: "Call unto Me, and I will answer thee, and show thee great and mighty things, which thou knowest not."*
> —Jeremiah 33:3

2. Don't lean on your own understanding.

God's path may not always look appealing—but it leads to life. My shortcut led me through hidden mud that left me filthy and exhausted. His way would've spared me.

> *Scripture: "Trust in the Lord with all thine heart; and lean not unto thine own understanding. In all thy ways acknowledge Him, and He shall direct thy paths"*
> —Proverbs 3:5–6.

3. Jesus says, "Come unto Me and I will give you rest."

After I obeyed, He led me to water—where I washed, waited, and rested.

> *Scripture: "Come unto Me, all ye that labour and are heavy laden, and I will give you rest."*
> —Matthew 11:28

194

4. Even when you think the trail ends, follow Him.

"I am the way, the truth, and the life." He always makes a way.

Scripture: "Jesus saith unto him, I am the way, the truth, and the life: no man cometh unto the Father, but by Me"
—John 14:6.

5. We've come too far to turn back.

Still, God honors our free will. Keep going forward in faith.

Scripture: "But Jesus said unto him, No man, having put his hand to the plough, and looking back, is fit for the kingdom of God"
—Luke 9:62.

6. You can't—but God can.

"Trust Me, Jeff." Those words reminded me that my strength fails—but His never does.

Scripture: "With men this is impossible; but with God all things are possible"
—Matthew 19:26.

7. "The Lord is good, a stronghold in the day of trouble..."

When I let go, He held me up.

Scripture: "The Lord is good, a stronghold in the day of trouble; and He knoweth them that trust in Him"
—Nahum 1:7.

8. How much of the Holy Spirit do you want?

Ankle-deep? Waist-deep? Or will you step under the waterfall?

> *Scripture: "Afterward he measured... the waters were to the ankles... to the knees... to the loins... waters to swim in, a river that could not be passed over"*
> —Ezekiel 47:3–5.

9. "I will never leave you nor forsake you."

Just when I needed water, a young man appeared—like an angel from Heaven.

> *Scripture: "For He hath said, I will never leave thee, nor forsake thee"*
> —Hebrews 13:5.

10. One step of obedience at a time.

When I returned to the muddy path, I trusted God. This time, I saw the stepping stones—and walked through clean.

> *Scripture: "Order my steps in Thy word: and let not any iniquity have dominion over me"*
> —Psalm 119:133.

The mountain didn't just teach me how to walk—it taught me how to follow. Not with my eyes on the trail, but with my heart fixed on the One who leads it. And every step of obedience, no matter how small, becomes part of something far bigger than we can imagine.

When we walk by faith, the stepping stones appear.

One at a time.

Just in time.

Reflection

There is a path prepared for every obedient heart—one that doesn't always make sense on a map but always leads to deeper intimacy with God. Sometimes it looks like a muddy trail. Sometimes it feels like a risk. But when we trust the Lord and step forward in faith, He reveals the way, one stone at a time. What may seem uncertain in the moment becomes sacred in hindsight. The Lord does not waste a single step. He trains our ears to hear His voice, our hearts to trust His plan, and our feet to follow—even through the unknown. Each trial, each test, becomes a testimony. Each act of obedience, a stone of remembrance.

Wherever you are right now—on the mountain or in the mud—know this: if you're following Jesus, you're on the right path.

Scripture

"And thine ears shall hear a word behind thee, saying, This is the way, walk ye in it, when ye turn to the right hand, and when ye turn to the left"

—Isaiah 30:21

Prayer

Father, thank You for the journey, even when the trail is steep and the way is unclear. Thank You for every stone, every stream, every whisper that has brought me closer to You. Teach me to trust You not just on the mountaintop but in the mud, not just when the way is clear but when the next step is hidden. Help me to walk by faith, one obedient step at a time. Let my life be a testimony of Your goodness, and may every step lead others closer to Your heart. In Jesus' name, Amen.

CHAPTER 21

The Shade, the Shepherd, and the Summit

A Day That Began with a Whisper

Some days begin with a destination. Others begin with a whisper. That morning, I had no schedule, no appointments, and no one expecting me—just a rented mountain bike, an open sky, and a stirring in my spirit. It was the kind of morning where the wind feels like a nudge from Heaven and the road ahead feels like an invitation. I wasn't chasing a trail—I was following the Lord.

With every turn of the pedal, I felt the Lord guiding me, not with loud direction but with gentle assurance. I didn't know where I was going—but I knew Who was leading.

This chapter is a story of unexpected turns, divine encounters, and the quiet ways God speaks when we have no plan but to follow. It's about a tree in the middle of a sun-scorched field, a voice in the dark, and the kind of moments that make you stop and say, *"Only God."*

Little did I know, the journey I was about to take would lead me not just through valleys and mountain roads but also straight into the heart of God's perfect timing.

The Shade in the Valley

The next morning, I rented a mountain bike from the hostel and set off toward the northeast. The sky above was a deep, brilliant blue, and though the sun was already hot, a gentle breeze pressed against my back—as if the Lord Himself was urging me onward.

The trail dipped into a steep path and opened into a wide, golden valley. At its center stood a mighty tree, its branches outstretched like welcoming arms. I parked the bike, walked beneath the vast canopy, and found sweet rest beneath its limbs.

In that shade, the temperature dropped dramatically—at least twenty degrees cooler. I whispered a prayer for a cool breeze, and right then, God sent it. No words can fully capture the moment. I danced a little, prayed a little, and thanked Him out loud, because I knew He was right there with me. If anyone had seen me, they might've thought I'd lost my mind—but I hadn't. I had simply found peace.

Stepping out from under that tree, the heat came rushing back in full force. But under its covering, there was peace, rest, and refreshing wind. It reminded me of a parable of Jesus:

> *"Abide in me, and I in you. As the branch cannot bear fruit of itself, except it abide in the vine; no more can ye, except ye abide in me"*
>
> —John 15:4.

Land Mines and a Barking Dog

After resting, I pressed on, climbing a steep incline and pushing the bike with determination. At the top, a gravel road forced a choice—left or right. I chose right. Before long, I reached a wire fence with a sign that stopped me in my tracks:

"Land Mines – Do Not Enter."

That was all the convincing I needed to turn around.

Backtracking, I noticed a narrow dirt trail branching off the road. I left the bike behind and continued on foot, camera in hand. In the distance, I spotted a beautiful pool of water and made my way through the brush to reach it. But as I drew near, I saw a large crowd—and every face turned to look at me.

Suddenly, a dog appeared behind me, barking aggressively. This wasn't just noise. It was hostile—almost demonic. I prayed, *"Lord, if this dog bites me, I'll do what I have to do. But if I do, I'll have a problem with this crowd. Please make it stop and return to its owner."* Instantly, the barking ceased, and the dog walked away. Just like that. Another "wow" moment with God.

Part of me wanted to retreat. But I felt the Lord urging me to stand tall. So I walked right into the crowd, took the photo I had come for, smiled, and said, "Hello! How are you all doing?" Then I turned and walked back through them—completely at peace.

Streams in the Valley

On the return trail, I met a young man coming the opposite way. He told me about another spot farther down—a quieter place with fewer people. I thanked him and followed his directions, only to realize I had circled back to the same spot with the land mine warning. But this time, something caught my eye—a new trail branching off to the right. No fence. No signs.

I followed it.

The path led into a lush, green valley, like a living tunnel made of trees and brush. Eventually, I came to a brook and a small waterfall. I sat there by the water, completely alone, listening to the gentle sound of the stream, sitting under the shade once again. Peace settled over me like a warm blanket.

I thought about the simplicity of walking with God. His paths may not always look safe, but they always lead somewhere sacred. The world may say we're alone—but Jesus said:

"I will never leave thee, nor forsake thee.
—Hebrews 13:5.

I believed that promise.

As I biked back to the hostel, I was overwhelmed by the presence of the Holy Spirit. He truly is the Helper Jesus promised—teaching, guiding, and protecting me every step of the way. I finally understood what Paul meant:

"I am crucified with Christ: nevertheless I live; yet not I, but Christ liveth in me"
—Galatians 2:20.

The Road to Tiberias

The next day, I began my journey toward Tiberias. I caught a bus to the Hula Valley in Northern Galilee and hiked into a nature reserve. Once again, I had no itinerary—just me and Jesus. I walked up a country road that reminded me of home in Kentucky.

When I reached the reserve, I was stunned. The scenery was breathtaking. Thousands of birds migrate through this area each year. I thought of Joshua, David, and especially Jesus. How many battles were fought here? How many feet had walked this very land?

That evening, I stood at a roadside bus stop. A bus picked me up and carried me toward Tiberias as the sun began to set over the Sea of Galilee. It was beautiful—golden light dancing on the waves.

A Voice in the Dark

I wanted to go to Mount Arbel, but I didn't know if there were places to stay nearby. The attendant explained it was a national park with no lodging, but a bus to a nearby village was about to leave.

I boarded.

As the bus emptied, only an elderly woman and I remained. When she prepared to get off, she turned and walked back toward me.

"Where are you going?" she asked gently.

I told her I was trying to get to Mount Arbel and needed a place to sleep. She gave me directions, but I didn't know the area or the street names.

At the next stop, she walked to the front of the bus and spoke firmly to the driver, then pointed at me. When she exited, I moved up front. A moment later, the driver pointed behind us, then at me, then at himself, and then ahead. I got the message: he would let me off up ahead, but I needed to walk back to that road.

I got off and walked back in total darkness. No lights. No people. Just trees and dirt. I couldn't even see my hand in front of my face.

Then—out of nowhere—a voice spoke:

"Go through the gate."

I never saw anyone. Just a voice.

I reached out, and sure enough, there was a gate.

"Yes, that gate," the voice said again, sounding like it came from the middle of the roadway.

How did the person know that I only spoke English?

I stepped through and walked toward a distant light. As I drew closer, I saw a small family restaurant—and, to my amazement, a place to stay. A man greeted me as I walked through the doorway. He spoke English and explained that they had converted his grandmother's home into a hostel.

That's where I stayed for the next week.

The Frenchman and the Priest

The next day, I met a man from France. His English was rough, so I slowed my words to help him understand. When I told him I was from Kentucky, he grinned, squinted, and said, "I knew it! You are from the South!" Then he tried to mimic my accent—not very well—but I got the point.

He was mocking my heritage, the place that shaped me.

Now, I've learned to be spiritually alert when I meet people on these journeys. I believe God sends people to me—and sends me to people. But at that moment, I turned to the Lord in quiet frustration and said, *"I'm done with this man. You deal with him."*

Later that evening, I went into the hostel's common area, laid my Bible and tablet on the coffee table, and began reading about the Transfiguration of Jesus. Some believe it happened on Mount Hermon, but I—like many others—believe it happened on Mount Tabor. To me, the timeline makes sense. Jesus had taken His disciples from Caesarea Philippi, and six days later, they were on the mountain with Moses and Elijah. Mount Hermon was too close. Tabor was a more likely match.

I knew that's where I wanted to go next, though I didn't know how I'd get there. Renting a car felt wrong without the Lord's release. Buses were too slow, and taxis were too expensive. So, I waited.

It was nearly 10 p.m. when the Frenchman returned to the common room. He paused, looked at me, and asked with a furrowed brow,

"Why do you do this?"

Right then, the Holy Spirit nudged my heart:

"Pack up everything. Even My Word. Give this man your full attention."

I obeyed. I closed the Bible, powered down my tablet, and looked him in the eye.

"Sorry," I said gently. "I was just studying Scripture, trying to decide where to go tomorrow. I read the Bible and then go to the places I've read about."

He paused. Then he said something that surprised me:

"Come outside. Talk with me and... the priest."

I jumped up. "Absolutely," I said. "Give me one moment." I packed up my things, placed them on my cot, and stepped out into the cool night air.

There, under the stars, sat the Frenchman and a German priest at a table.

A Father's Grief

As I joined them, the Frenchman looked at me with searching eyes and asked,

"Tell me—why would God take my nine-year-old daughter from me?"

My heart sank. I silently cried out to the Lord for wisdom. This was no small question—this was the ache of a father's soul.

"What man knows the mind of God?" I replied. "But this I do know: your daughter is with God. And if you and I live godly lives, we will one day be with her again."

He listened. I could tell my words pierced deep—not because they were eloquent, but because they were true.

Throughout the conversation, he would pause to ask the priest for help translating my answers. From that moment on, he never again mocked my accent.

The laughter had turned to longing.

The discussion turned to prayer. I said, *"A prayerless man is a powerless man."* I told them about the miracles I'd experienced—how God had healed me, how He had just healed my neighbor.

The German priest looked at me and asked,

"So... you pray one-on-one with God?"

I smiled. "Yes, sir. That's exactly how it works."

I explained how all believers are priests. Jesus is our High Priest, our Mediator, and our Intercessor.

"For there is one God, and one mediator between God and men, the man Christ Jesus"

—1 Timothy 2:5.

Before we parted ways that night, the German priest said he would begin encouraging personal prayer in his church. I was in awe of how God had turned the evening around.

The Frenchman then turned to me and said,

"Jeff, I have a rental car for one more day. I have no plans tomorrow. Where would you like to go?"

I didn't even hesitate. "Mount Tabor."

On the Mountain of Transfiguration

The next morning, we set off together. On the drive, the Frenchman asked, "Do you feel anything when you visit the holy places?" "Yes," I said. "Most of the time, I do."

He nodded slowly and admitted, "I never have." I could see the pain and confusion still hiding behind his eyes. He needed a touch from God that no words could provide.

It was a picture-perfect day—blue skies, cool breeze. We parked on top of Mount Tabor near the entrance of the Church of the Transfiguration and walked the narrow road to the church site.

When we arrived, the atmosphere shifted. The air was light. The Church of the Transfiguration stood in silent reverence. As we walked through it, I could feel the Holy Spirit moving.

At the overlook, the Frenchman stood silently, then turned toward me—smiling. It was a soft, holy moment. God had begun to move in his heart.

On the way back, we talked more about life, faith, and the mystery of grief. Before we parted ways, he said again,

"Remember me in your prayers."

And I have.

205

That evening, the three of us sat outside once more— the Frenchman, the priest, and I. He asked again,

"Please, keep me in your prayers."

We promised we would.

The Heights of Arbel

The next few days were spent exploring Mount Arbel. I believe this could very well be the mountain where Jesus gave the Great Commission. Scripture doesn't name it, but from the heights of Arbel, you can see nearly the whole Galilee region.

I imagined Jesus pointing out over the hills, teaching His disciples and all of those who pass by, who would stop and listen: *Do you remember when I called you there? Do you remember the miracles? Now I send you."*

"Go ye into all the world, and preach the gospel to every creature"
—Mark 16:15.

When my time there ended, I returned to Tiberias by bus. As I stepped off, something stirred in my spirit:

"You're finished with the buses."

I didn't fully understand what that meant—but I knew it was God.

A New Way Forward

That night, I stayed one last time in Tiberias. The next morning, I set out walking—full stride, like I knew where I was going. Truthfully, I had no idea.

Then, out of nowhere, a woman approached me and began speaking fluent Greek. I smiled, captivated by the language—even though I didn't understand a word.

You see, I only speak English. But her voice reminded me of my wife, Anissa. She, too, only knows English—yet when she prays, she speaks in tongues, a Heavenly language. It's a gift from God. Listening to that woman brought that gift to mind.

When she finished, I asked, "Do you speak English?" She waved me off and walked away.

I kept walking, turned up a side road, over a hill—and there it was.

A Hertz car rental.

I walked in and asked, "Do you have anything available?"

The lady behind the counter smiled. "We only have one car left."

Of course they did.

I rented the car and began driving across Galilee. I thought to myself—if I had rented that car earlier, I would have missed the Frenchman, the priest, the mountain, and everything God had planned in between.

Reflection

This chapter was more than a journey across Galilee—it was a journey deeper into trust. A tree's shade, a hostile dog silenced, a voice in the dark, a grieving father, and a holy mountain—every step was a reminder that God orders the path of His children.

When we don't have a plan, His plan unfolds. When we don't know the way, His voice whispers, *"Go through the gate."* When our strength falters, His Spirit renews us. Even in our frustrations with people, God has a way of turning mockery into ministry and questions into encounters.

This journey showed me that obedience isn't always about knowing where you are going—it's about knowing Who goes with you.

Scripture

"Trust in the Lord with all thine heart; and lean not unto thine own understanding. In all thy ways acknowledge him, and he shall direct thy paths"

—Proverbs 3:5–6.

Prayer

Lord, I thank You for the shade You provide in dry places, for the still waters in hidden valleys, and for the gentle voice that guides me in the dark. Teach me to walk by faith and not by sight, to trust Your timing, and to obey even when the way is unclear. May my life bear witness to Your faithfulness, and may every step I take point others to Jesus. Amen.

CHAPTER 22

The Road of Revelation: From Galilee to Jerusalem

After renting the car, I felt an overwhelming sense of freedom—like the weight of limitations had suddenly been lifted. No more bus schedules, no more waiting on strangers. I could now drive anywhere the Spirit led me. And that's exactly what I did.

I started by circling the entire Sea of Galilee, taking in the views I had once walked and now drove. My first stop was Magdala, the hometown of Mary Magdalene. The archaeological site here is relatively new, discovered just in the last couple of decades, but what they've uncovered is stunning—stone roads, a first-century synagogue that Jesus Himself likely walked through, and the remnants of a vibrant fishing village. As I stood there, I imagined Mary encountering Jesus for the first time—broken, possessed, and yet chosen. This was where transformation began.

From there, I headed north to Capernaum, the town Jesus called His own during His Galilean ministry. Walking those ancient streets again, I passed by the ruins of Peter's house and the synagogue where Jesus taught with authority. This wasn't just a biblical footnote—it was real, tangible, and still echoing with the footsteps of the Messiah. The Scripture came alive again:

"And leaving Nazareth, he came and dwelt in Capernaum... that it might be fulfilled which was spoken by Esaias the prophet."

—Matthew 4:13–14

Next, I drove to Tabgha, the traditional site of the miraculous multiplication of loaves and fish. A beautiful mosaic marks the spot, picturing two fish and a basket of bread. It was peaceful there. Birds chirped in the background, and the water lapped gently against the shore. I couldn't help but think how a little boy's offering—insignificant in human eyes—fed thousands in the hands of Jesus. Sometimes, God doesn't need more from us... He just needs all of us.

I continued east and stopped at Kursi *(Traditionally identified as the land of the Gadarenes (or Gerasenes) mentioned in the Gospels (Matthew 8:28–34; Mark 5:1–20; Luke 8:26–39),* the site believed to be where Jesus cast the legion of demons into a herd of swine (Mark 5). Overlooking the eastern shore, the land drops steeply—just as the Scripture says that the pigs rushed down the hill into the water. Standing there, I thought about the authority Jesus carried. Even demons had to bow at His presence. And the man who had been tormented became a witness to his entire region, testifying of God's mercy.

From there, I slowly cruised along the edge of the lake, pulling over frequently just to sit and take it all in. Somewhere along these shores, Jesus walked on water. Somewhere near, He calmed the storm. It struck me that over 70% of His recorded miracles occurred right here around the Sea of Galilee. The place where Heaven touched Earth... again and again.

"And great multitudes came unto him, having with them those that were lame, blind, dumb, maimed, and many others, and cast them down at Jesus' feet; and he healed them"

—Matthew 15:30.

The next day, I drove north—deep into the Golan Heights, nearing the borders of Lebanon and Syria. The terrain changed. The land became more rugged, the altitude higher. Eventually, I reached Caesarea Philippi, where Jesus once asked His disciples:

"But whom say ye that I am?"
—Matthew 16:15.

This region was known for pagan worship—temples carved into rock faces, idols dedicated to the god Pan, and rituals carried out in front of what the locals called "the gates of Hell." And yet, right there, in the heart of spiritual darkness, Jesus declared:

"Upon this rock I will build my church; and the gates of hell shall not prevail against it"
—Matthew 16:18.

To be there, in that place where light confronted darkness and truth was proclaimed with eternal authority—it was powerful.

Just a short drive away—about seven miles—I arrived at Biblical Dan. This area, rich with water from the headwaters of the Jordan River, was once home to one of the ancient northern tribes of Israel. The site includes remnants of the city gate from the time of Abraham, as well as the altar and high places set up by Jeroboam after the kingdom split.

"Whereupon the king took counsel, and made two calves of gold... And he set the one in Bethel, and the other put he in Dan"
—1 Kings 12:28–29.

I walked through the shaded paths and ancient stones of Dan, feeling the contrast between God's original design for His people and the compromise that took place here. Yet even in such a place, God's creation flourished. Streams of living water bubbled up and flowed freely—reminding me that where man fails, God still moves.

After exploring the Upper Galilee and the Golan Heights, I continued my journey by car—this time heading west toward the Mediterranean. My next stop was the ancient coastal city of Acre, also known as Akko. The moment I entered the city, I felt like I had stepped into a living museum. The salty sea air, the narrow stone streets, and the echoes of centuries gone by filled the atmosphere.

Acre has been inhabited for thousands of years. It was once a key port city for the Phoenicians and later a stronghold for the Crusaders. I walked through its ancient halls, tunnels, and fortresses, imagining the waves of history that had swept through this place—Romans, Byzantines, Crusaders, and Ottomans. Though it's not directly tied to any one moment in Jesus' ministry, standing at the edge of the Mediterranean, I thought about how far the gospel would travel from these shores—to the ends of the earth.

> *"But I say, Have they not heard? Yes verily, their sound went into all the earth, and their words unto the ends of the world"*
>
> —Romans 10:18.

From Acre, I turned south and drove down the stunning coastline to the ruins of Caesarea Maritima. Built by Herod the Great, Caesarea was once the grand Roman capital of Judea. Here stood an amphitheater, a massive harbor, a racetrack, and the remains of Herod's palace. This was the place where the apostle Paul was imprisoned for two years before being sent to Rome.

As I walked the stone paths along the coast, I thought about Paul's boldness—his willingness to stand before kings and governors, unashamed of the gospel. It was here he stood before Festus and Agrippa and declared:

"Whereupon, O king Agrippa, I was not disobedient unto the heavenly vision"

—Acts 26:19.

The sea crashed against the ancient ruins, but the message of Christ still echoed stronger than the waves. I stood there, soaking in the magnitude of what had once happened in that very place—God using a Roman courtroom to launch the gospel further west.

After leaving Caesarea, I made my way back inland and north toward Chorazin. Along with Capernaum and Bethsaida, Chorazin was one of the three cities Jesus rebuked for their unbelief, despite the miracles He had performed among them. The ruins of Chorazin sit high above the Sea of Galilee, made mostly of dark basalt stone. As I wandered through the remains of homes and the ancient synagogue, I thought about what Jesus said:

"Woe unto thee, Chorazin! woe unto thee, Bethsaida! for if the mighty works, which were done in you, had been done in Tyre and Sidon, they would have repented long ago in sackcloth and ashes"

—Matthew 11:21.

It was a sobering moment to stand where Jesus once taught and realize that people still chose to reject Him. I prayed right then and there: "Lord, may I never take Your Word for granted. May I always believe when You speak."

From Chorazin, I decided to venture farther northeast toward the ancient site of Bethsaida. But when I arrived, I quickly realized something wasn't quite right. Archaeologists believe the site currently marked as Bethsaida—also known as et-Tell—may not actually be the biblical Bethsaida of the Gospels. It's located quite a distance from the Sea of Galilee, making it unlikely that Peter, Andrew, and Philip— fishermen by trade—would have lived that far from the water.

There is ongoing debate among scholars and archaeologists about the true location of Bethsaida. Some believe it lies elsewhere, closer to the shoreline. But even if this wasn't the exact spot, the surrounding area still echoed with the memory of the Messiah. After all, it was near Bethsaida that Jesus restored sight to a blind man (Mark 8), and it was the hometown of several of His disciples.

It reminded me: even if I stood slightly off from the "exact" location, I was still within the very region where Jesus had walked, healed, taught, and called His disciples to follow Him. Whether or not I stood on the exact stone where a miracle occurred didn't matter as much as the truth that His presence had saturated this land. The specifics of geography fade in the light of spiritual truth—Jesus was here, and more importantly, He is still calling hearts to follow Him today.

> *"And he saith unto them, Follow me, and I will make you fishers of men"*
> —Matthew 4:19.

The following day, I returned to the peaceful hostel near Mount Arbel, where I had stayed earlier during my unexpected but divine encounter with the Frenchman and the priest. I spent the next three days there, resting, reflecting, and walking in awe of what the Lord had already done—and what He was still teaching me.

Though Mount Arbel is not directly mentioned in connection with the Great Commission, or even explicitly named in the Gospels as a site of Jesus' specific teachings, it has long been believed by many to be one of the "high places" where Jesus would retreat to pray and teach His disciples. The Scriptures frequently mention that Jesus went up into the mountains, often alone or with His closest followers, especially in the region surrounding Galilee.

"And when he had sent the multitudes away, he went up into a mountain apart to pray: and when the evening was come, he was there alone"

—Matthew 14:23.

As I stood atop Mount Arbel, I could see the layout of history spread out beneath me—the rolling Galilean hills, the surrounding villages, the fields where wheat once grew and parables were spoken, and the roads where dusty feet carried the Gospel from town to town. I imagined Jesus standing there with His disciples, pointing across the land:

"Do you remember when I called you from there?
Do you remember the miracles that happened over there?
Now, I give you this charge..."

"Go ye therefore, and teach all nations, baptizing them in the name of the Father, and of the Son, and of the Holy Ghost: Teaching them to observe all things whatsoever I have commanded you: and, lo, I am with you alway, even unto the end of the world. Amen"

—Matthew 28:19–20.

I reflected on the many "mountaintop moments" of my journey. God had orchestrated every step—even the ones I didn't understand at the time. Mount Arbel became more than just a hilltop; it became a symbol. A reminder that Jesus commissions us from places of intimacy with Him—from places of elevation, yes, but also from places of revelation.

He calls us not just to see the view, but to go down from the mountain and carry the message. And in that calling, He promises His presence—not just in Galilee, but everywhere we go.

That evening, as the sun lowered itself over the quiet waters of the Sea of Galilee, a deep stillness came over me. I stood at the shore one final time, letting the breeze brush across my face and the memories of

215

the past days wash over me like the gentle waves at my feet. It was hard to believe—but my time here had come to an end.

I took a long, reflective walk, thanking the Lord for everything: the bike ride through the valley, the divine appointments, the miracle of Mount Arbel, the lessons from ancient stones, and the voice that had guided me in the dark. Galilee had been more than a place—it had been a classroom, a sanctuary, and a turning point.

The next morning, I returned the rental car, packed up my things, and caught a bus headed south toward Jerusalem. This wasn't just the end of my Galilean journey—it was the final stretch of a mission that began long before my feet ever touched Israeli soil. Five days remained, and I knew the Lord still had more to show me.

As the bus rolled through the terrain, something stirred in my heart. It wasn't sadness. It wasn't anxiety. It was completion—a knowing that I had walked the path the Lord had laid before me. Not perfectly, but obediently. Not always confidently, but faithfully.

When I arrived in Jerusalem, something familiar welcomed me before I even got off the bus. The energy. The weight. The holiness of the city. Jerusalem isn't like any other place on earth. It carries a spiritual gravity—like time slows and Heaven leans in a little closer. It's where God chose to place His Name.

I returned to the same hostel I had stayed at during my previous trip, tucked just off Jaffa Street. As I walked through the door, the manager looked up from the front desk and grinned.

"Hello, Kentucky," he said with a warm smile.

I laughed. "Yep. *I'm back home.*"

There's something about being remembered in a foreign land. I didn't need to explain who I was. No need to introduce myself or give a backstory. Just "Kentucky." And that was enough.

After checking in, I made my way to the same cot I had slept on during my last visit—like a returning soldier to a familiar barracks. I dropped my backpack, took a deep breath, and then quietly stepped into the common area, Bible in hand.

There, in the holiest city on earth, I opened the Word of God and began to read.

The Scriptures felt alive in a way that's hard to explain. Not just text on a page—but living words, spoken in the very streets outside the hostel walls. The stories I read weren't distant—they were rooted in the stones of the city. I wasn't just reading about Jesus walking into Jerusalem—I was sitting in the city He wept over, taught in, suffered in, and rose again from.

> *"O Jerusalem, Jerusalem, thou that killest the prophets, and stonest them which are sent unto thee, how often would I have gathered thy children together, even as a hen gathereth her chickens under her wings, and ye would not!"*
> —Matthew 23:37.

There in that little common room, surrounded by strangers and noise, I found a pocket of stillness. I studied. I prayed. And I thanked God for bringing me back—not just physically to Jerusalem, but spiritually to a deeper place of surrender, purpose, and understanding.

Five days remained. And though I didn't know what they held, I knew Who held them.

Reflection

The road from Galilee to Jerusalem is more than geography—it is a spiritual journey every believer must walk. Galilee speaks of calling, miracles, and revelation; Jerusalem speaks of surrender, sacrifice, and destiny. Jesus Himself walked this path, setting His face toward Jerusalem, knowing what awaited Him there. In my own journey, I saw how each site whispered the same truth: God is always preparing us for the next step. The mountaintops remind us of His presence, but it is in the valleys and the crowded cities where His mission is fulfilled.

Galilee taught me to see, but Jerusalem was calling me to believe, obey, and carry the testimony forward. The lessons of revelation are not meant to stay on the mountain—they are meant to be lived out in the place where the cross meets the world.

Scripture

"For whatsoever things were written aforetime were written for our learning, that we through patience and comfort of the scriptures might have hope"
—Romans 15:4.

"The grass withereth, the flower fadeth: but the word of our God shall stand for ever"
—Isaiah 40:8.

Prayer

Lord, thank You for revealing Yourself in both quiet places and ancient ruins. Thank You for the lessons carved in stone, the whispers in the wilderness, and the truth that Your Word endures forever. Teach me to walk humbly, listen closely, and trust fully—whether I stand in the sanctuary of Galilee or the silence of Petra. Shape my life as You shaped these lands, with purpose, mercy, and eternal vision. In Jesus' name, Amen.

CHAPTER 23

The Journey Continues

Some journeys don't end when the road runs out. They shift. They stretch. They deepen.

When I left Jerusalem for the final time on that trip, I knew I wasn't the same man who had arrived weeks before with no itinerary and only faith to guide me. God had wrecked me—in the best way possible. He had stripped me of control, filled me with wonder, and showed me what it meant to truly walk with Him.

But as the bus pulled away and the hills of Galilee faded into memory, I felt something I didn't expect.

Not an ending. A beginning.

You see, the journey didn't stop when I left Galilee or passed through the gates of Jerusalem. It continued. It still does. Because the story God is writing isn't bound to geography or time. It lives in the heart of every believer who dares to follow Jesus without a map.

Since that trip, I've seen God move in ways that still leave me speechless. He's opened doors I never could've forced open myself. He's healed relationships, answered prayers, and called me into rooms I didn't feel worthy to enter. I've met people who said, "I needed to hear that." And more than anything, I've realized this life of walking by faith isn't a one-time event—it's a daily invitation.

An invitation to surrender. To obey. To go. Even when you don't know where you're going.

219

That's what I hope this book has stirred in your heart—not just a fascination with Israel or the miracles of the Bible, but a hunger to know the Author of it all, personally. Jesus isn't just a figure in history. He's alive. And He's still calling people to follow Him—one step at a time.

You don't need a passport to encounter Him. You don't need to stand on the Mount of Olives to hear His whisper. You just need a heart that's willing to say, "Here I am, Lord. Send me."

This chapter marks the close of this book, but not the end of the story. The journey continues—both for me and, I pray, for you. And yes, I'll be writing more. Not because I want to build a platform or tell another story—but because I believe God's not finished yet.

There are still lessons to learn. Still deserts to cross.

Still strangers to meet, and gates in the dark to walk through.

Wherever He leads, I'll follow. And I hope you will too.

Let's keep walking.

In my final nights in Israel, as I reflected on everything God had done, I stumbled upon a YouTube video by Dr. Todd Michael Fink. He was teaching a biblical lesson right there in Jerusalem—on the very streets where I had just walked. As I listened, my heart stirred:

"I've got to meet this man of God. I haven't found another teacher who so clearly exalts Jesus instead of self."

Not long after, God arranged it. I met Todd—and soon became friends not only with him, but also with his wife, Letsy, and their two sons, Joel and Logan. I'll never forget the first time I shook his hand. With genuine humility, he smiled and said, *"You can just call me Todd."*

That introduction marked the beginning of a lasting friendship with a gifted pastor and teacher who truly loves Jesus. In time, I would take a couple of tours with him and even return to Israel many more times—including a 40-day and 40-night stay throughout the land, walking and praying for Israel.

Many people may never be able to make the trip to Israel themselves, but my good friend Todd can take you there through the many videos he and his family have created. You can explore these resources on his website at **holylandsite.com** or by visiting his **HolyLandSite YouTube channel**, where biblical truth and the land of the Bible come alive.

Afterwards, the war began. Little did I know what was about to unfold—but God did.

Reflection

The journey did not end when I boarded the plane home, nor when I closed my Bible at the hostel in Jerusalem. The journey continues—because God's calling is never finished. He places people in our lives, like Todd and his family, to encourage us, teach us, and walk beside us in faith. He opens doors we never expect and carries us into places we could never go on our own. Though wars may come and uncertainty may fill the land, the Word of God remains sure. And just as He led me through valleys, mountaintops, and ancient stones, He will lead me home!

Scripture

"Faithful is he that calleth you, who also will do it"
—1 Thessalonians 5:24.

Prayer

Lord, thank You for this journey—for the teachings and the friendships You ordained along the way. Thank You for Todd and his family, for the gift of fellowship in Your truth. As the days grow darker and the nations rage, help me to keep walking by faith, trusting that You will finish the work You have begun. May my life, like this book, be a testimony that points others to Jesus until the very end. Amen.

Final Word

Walk With Me and Jesus... One More Step

I didn't write this book to impress you.
I wrote it to invite you.

Not to a religion.
Not to a destination.
But to a walk with Jesus—real, raw, and unrelenting.

Every road in these pages led to one truth:
He is Who He says He is.

We all need a Savior.
He is that Savior.
The Lamb of God.
The Risen King.
The One Who took our place.

Are you broken?
He is the Potter—
and He makes all things new.

Are you weary?
He is Rest for your soul
and Peace that passes understanding.

Are you sick?
He is the Healer,
the Great Physician who still touches today.

Are you bound?
He is the Deliverer.
The Chain-Breaker.
The Freedom-Giver.

Are you lost?
He is the Way,
the Truth,
and the Life.

Are you afraid?
He is your Refuge,
your Rock,
your Fortress in the storm.

Do you feel unseen?
He is El Roi—
the God who sees you
and never looks away.

Do you need a miracle?
He is the Miracle Worker,
the same yesterday,
today,
and forever.

Do you need a friend?
He is a Friend
that sticks closer than a brother.

Do you long to be loved?
He is Love itself—
perfect,

unshakable,
everlasting.

I've sat with strangers who became brothers.
Crossed borders where others saw only danger.
Worshiped in deserts.
Prayed on mountaintops.
And at every turn—
He met me there.

This isn't the end of the journey.
It's only the next step.

If you're wondering if God still leads…
He does.

If you're questioning whether He still speaks…
He does.

If you're afraid to take that next step…
take it anyway.

He'll meet you there.

*"He which testifieth these things saith, Surely I come quickly.
Amen. Even so, come, Lord Jesus"*
—Revelation 22:20.

Come.
Follow the whisper.
Take the next step.
Walk with Me and Jesus.

—J.W. Cromer

225

Closing Prayer of Blessing

Father in Heaven,

I thank You for every reader
who has walked through these pages.
May the seeds of faith planted here
grow deep roots in their hearts.
Lead them in Your ways,
strengthen them in their trials,
and fill them with the joy of Your presence.

Bless their homes,
their families,
their work,
and their walk with You.
Let Your Word be a lamp unto their feet
and a light unto their path.

When they feel weak,
be their strength.
When they are afraid,
be their peace.
When they are weary,
be their rest.
And when they feel alone,
remind them that You are always near.

Now unto Him
Who is able to keep us from falling,
and to present us faultless
before the presence of His glory
with exceeding joy—

May Jesus Christ be their Shepherd,
their Savior,
and their Song
until the journey is complete.

In His holy name I pray—
Amen.

"Follow the whisper. Take the next step. Walk with Jesus."
—J.W. Cromer

Made in the USA
Middletown, DE
29 November 2025

23550133R00144